The Right Moves, Volume II

The Right Moves, Volume II

Also By Ann C. Humphries

The Right Moves, Volume 1

The Door Swings Both Ways

The Door Swings Both Ways,
a video with South Carolina Educational Television.

For more information, contact ETICON, Etiquette Consultants for Business, P.O. Box 69530, Columbia, South Carolina 29223-8809 or call 803-736-1934.

Copyright, 1995, ETICON, Etiquette Consultants for Business, Inc.

Edited by Dianne Berry and Tom Poland
Cover by Gemma Kerr

The Right Moves, Volume II

More Etiquette Strategies for Business

by

Ann Chadwell Humphries

of

ETICON

Etiquette Consultants for Business

The Right Moves, Volume II

Introduction

People can be their own worst enemies. Scott Hamilton, in commenting on the Winter Olympics of 1990 and 1994, said that Kristi Yamaguchi's strength was her lack of weakness.

When individuals and companies do not assess the sources of their success and where they can improve, they limit themselves. Business is hard enough to conduct. By continuing dated practices that offend others, you work against yourself.

I'm a student, not an expert. I continue to seek answers. I marvel at how some people just seem to know how to act. They seem confident in diverse situations and confident in themselves.

This second set of columns which date from 1990 to 1993 reflect my continuing search for how people do things well. I'm hopeful the subjects and the people who have shared their insights are as helpful to you as they were to me.

October 1994
Columbia, South Carolina   Ann C. Humphries

The Right Moves, Volume II

TABLE OF CONTENTS

Foreword   ix.

Dedication   xi.

Acknowledgements   xi.

Book Summary   xiv.

Right The First Time: *Managing The Impressions You Make*
   Etiquette's Business Advantages   Page 1
   Overcoming Shyness   Page 3
   Recruiting New Members   Page 5
   Take Care With Names   Page 7
   Preparing For Conventions—Part One   Page 9
   Attending Conventions—Part Two   Page 11
   The Rewards Of Patience   Page 13
   Beware A Hurried Manner   Page 15

A Sharper Image
   Dressing Down For Business   Page 17

The Right Moves, Volume II

When The Heat Is On — Page 19
Hat Etiquette — Page 21
The Sounds Of Business — Page 23

A Way With Words
A Way With Words — Page 25
Grammar And Pronunciation — Page 27
Telephone Skills — Page 29
Effective Presentations — Page 31
Telling Jokes Is No Joke — Page 33
Risk Telling The Truth — Page 35
An Encouraging Word — Page 37
Proposal Strategies — Page 39
Advising Management Of Changes — Page 41

Social Graces For Business Places
Company Party Manners — Page 43
Holiday Formalities — Page 45
Here's A Toast — Page 47
Table Manners — Page 49
Holiday Etiquette—Part One — Page 51
Holiday Etiquette—Part Two — Page 53
Flying The Red, White, And Blue — Page 55
The Business Art Of Gift-Giving — Page 57
Thank You Notes — Page 59

The Right Moves, Volume II

Dealing With Differences
Gender Etiquette In The Workplace — Page 61
Religious Diversity — Page 63
Holy Days — Page 65
Dealing With The Issue Of Age — Page 67
The Sensitivities Of Race — Page 69
Let's Be Peacemakers — Page 71

Going Global
Canadian Business Customs — Page 73
Doing Business German Style — Page 75
Style Matters In Latin America — Page 77
The Mexican Style Of Business — Page 79
Business, The Southern Way — Page 81
Broad Generalizations — Page 83

Dealing With Difficult People
Handling Nosy People — Page 85
Disagreeing With People — Page 87
Addressing Rude People — Page 89
Handling A Bully — Page 91
Dealing With Snipers — Page 93
Standing Your Ground — Page 95
Dealing With Upset People — Page 97

The Right Moves, Volume II

Excuses And Accountability — Page 99
Apologies—Receiving And Giving — Page 101

Company Manners
Admirable Workplace Behaviors For Employees — Page 103
Employee Expectations Of Managers — Page 105
When Leadership Changes — Page 107
Downsizing With Grace — Page 109
Families Who Work Together — Page 111
Mixing Friends With Business — Page 113
Working With And Respecting Suppliers — Page 115
Poor Morale—Learn From It — Page 117
The Benefits Of a Light Touch — Page 119
Graceful Transitions — Page 121
Retiring With Grace — Page 123
The Art Of Leaving — Page 125
Good Endings — Page 127

Foreword

In the short time since Ann Humphries published her first book on business and social etiquette, major trends in business have emerged. The world and workplace have become much more relationship oriented. Gone are the days when decisions could be made independently or by a handful of people who could dictate decisions to others. To be successful now, people must bridge relationship interests and create avenues through which relationships are forged.

And, in this era of team building and cooperation, consensus is the key and requires a lot more work than taking arbitrary actions. It requires communicating with people and creating an understanding from which decisions can be made.

And, because of the ease of communications and transportation, the definition of community is changing from one of geography to one based on common interests, as anyone who plugs into computer networks knows.

And, because of the need for companies to grow beyond their home borders, and opportunities with new markets that have only emerged since Ann's last book, the successful person must have a global perspective. Now, instead of dealing with an homogenous population of say, English-speaking Americans, the business landscape now involves any number of nationalities and a tapestry of cul-

The Right Moves, Volume II

tures. Etiquette and manners mean respect for other people and acceptance of their cultural background.

In this age of relationships and consensus, instantaneous communications and global decision making, knowing the right approach toward making connections is more important than it has ever been.

Ann Humphries' short but powerful columns are about building those relationships. Ann has been successful at delivering that message since she began ETICON and also writing a regular column for *The State* newspaper on business etiquette since 1988 which has attracted a worldwide audience. Ann's work will help you successfully navigate through these complex channels of communications. Her messages are written in a style that is easy to absorb. They even can be cut out and pinned to your bulletin board or refrigerator as a reminder before an important event.

And taken as a whole, they will broaden your level of understanding, allowing you to act with confidence without having to learn by "experience," otherwise known as mistakes. I highly recommend this book as a useful tool for success and enjoyment of life.

Fred Monk
Business Editor
The State
September 1994

The Right Moves, Volume II

Dedication

This book is dedicated to my wonderful family.

Acknowledgements

I'd like to thank a few people for helping me complete this book. The experience and the outcome have become greater than the sum of the parts.

To the people I've quoted, thank you for sharing your insights. To the papers, especially *The State*, in Columbia, South Carolina, who have regularly published my work, thank you for encouraging me and enduring the early days. To Dianne Berry and Tom Poland, I appreciate your tireless, professional coaching to ensure this book reflected its highest good. To Normanne Potter, thanks for her witty criticism and constant encouragement.

To my husband, Kirk, for keeping me safe and asking questions others wouldn't. To my parents for their good examples, my children for their support, and for all the people who, as best and worst examples, serve as a constant source of material.

WHAT OTHERS HAVE SAID ABOUT THE RIGHT MOVES VOLUME TWO

"In a time when the word 'nice' has fallen into ill repute, Ann Chadwell Humphries illustrates the need for professional etiquette and kindness. Her columns strike the right chord, using specific everyday examples of how the manners our parents taught us (or didn't) make life not only more pleasant in the marketplace, but also more effective."
LIBBY BERNARDIN, *author, The Stealing*

"Excellent and useful information! In today's business environment, it's 'The Right Moves' that will distinguish the leader of the 90's."
WARREN A. DARBY, *Vice President, South Carolina Electric &Gas*

"These succinct columns offer refreshing common sense. Ann's wisdom applies to life beyond the corporate world, reflecting values of courtesy, honesty, and commitment."
MARK YEMMA, *Business News Editor, Los Angeles Times*

"Our weekly 'Jobs' section receives great response whenever I run Ann's column. She always addresses relevant work issues, and her suggestions are effective for workers, managers, and job seekers. I've put her recommendations to work in my own job, and they do make a difference."
MAUREEN SCHLANGEN, *Publications Editor, Dayton Daily News*

QUOTES FROM NOTABLE SOUTH CAROLINIANS ABOUT THE RIGHT MOVES VOLUME ONE

"Ann's insights are timely and topical. Her columns are invaluable workplace tools."
EARL D. HEWLETTE, JR., *Managing Director, Destination Wild Dunes*

"Pragmatic, focused and relevant. Read a section everyday, then start over. By the third time, you'll know what to do in almost every situation."
DR. PETER MITCHELL, *President, Columbia College*

"I have found the articles in Ann's book to be informative, interesting and very helpful in dealing with both the problems and solutions that are a part of every business today."
BILL BRADSHAW, *Chairman, Team Vest*

"This book provides a down to earth, common sense approach to success in the business world...the qualities discussed in the book are applicable to everyday life."
CHIEF CHARLES P. AUSTIN, SR., *Chief of Police, City of Columbia*

"In this everchanging environment, good etiquette is a constant that will give you a competitive edge."
JAMES T. McLAWHORN, JR., *Columbia Urban League*

"Ann's practical approach to business etiquette transcends all cultures and speaks to the very basis of human relations."
ROBIN LANGSTON GORMAN,
Greater Columbia Chamber of Commerce

"As a former professional athlete I highly recommend The Right Moves. Ann Humphries has certainly demonstrated a genuine knowledge and understanding of what it takes to make an individual successful in business and everday life."
GEORGE ROGERS, *Heisman Trophy Winner*

"The business world has changed radically. Ann Humphries helps professionals through the confusing maze of etiquette in the '90's."
JAN COLLINS STUCKER, *Editor, Business and Economic Review*

"Even experienced people shine with the polish this book provides. Shows you ways to be more efficient and with demanding schedules every minute counts."
CONNIE GINSBERG, *Executive Director, Family Connection*
DR. LEON GINSBERG, *Carolina Research Professor, University of South Carolina*

THE RIGHT MOVES, VOLUME TWO

Many books, read once, forever after stay on the shelf. Not this book. This is a book meant to be used.

Between the covers of this book lies a storehouse of knowledge. What is here will smooth the way to success in your personal and business life.

Think of an etiquette dilemma you encounter from time to time. Maybe you hesitate when introducing people, or perhaps you'd like strategies to avoid feeling awkward, stilted, or just too eager at business receptions. You may ponder whether to tell employees that their appearance on "Casual Day" is just a little too casual. Or to avoid embarrassment to you or your organization, you'd like to know what religious holy days to avoid when scheduling business events.

Whatever your etiquette issue, thumb through the table of contents or index of this book. Chances are good that you'll find what you need, and the book's format makes it easy to access the information.

How does etiquette help business? The answers are so obvious that they are often overlooked. Etiquette builds your confidence for conducting business whether in familiar or unfamiliar, formal or informal settings. Etiquette helps you negotiate delicate professional relations with people who may be very different from you. And etiquette helps keep the atmosphere civil and somewhat structured, so that work can be accomplished.

Who doesn't need help now and then? Having this book at your office, in your brief case, or by your bedside is the same as having a team of consultants ready to answer questions or clarify issues. Take an afternoon to read it or pick it up for a quick tip.

Whether you want simple strategies on updating telephone techniques, how to address correspondence, advice for handling upset people, correcting grammar, or hand-holding while you negotiate race and gender issues at work, this book provides you with uncommon, common sense.

The Right Moves, Volume II

Right The First Time: Managing The Impressions You Make

Ann C. Humphries

Etiquette's Business Advantages

Etiquette can often provide the discipline to accomplish what might be unpleasant but necessary. Manners enable you to conduct business when the topic is uncomfortable or the process delicate. Manners discipline you to interact productively with people you do not like, with whom you might disagree or who have wronged you.

Having manners does not mean that you are avoiding difficult subjects for fear of hurting people's feelings or stirring up trouble. Nor does it mean that you always look on the bright side ("If you can't say anything nice...") or remain cheery when you should be angry. Forget the notion that manners take up too much time. They don't. They save it, and they protect the process that creates an environment where people can function at their peak.

Think of the people you know who have handled difficult situations well. Then, think of those who mishandled themselves in critical situations, who embarrassed your organization, who alienated not just customers, but fellow employees.

Ben Rast, financial adviser with Prudential-Bache and radio

Etiquette enables you to be comfortable and to put others at ease no matter what setting you are in.

talk show host said, "With etiquette, you avoid pitfalls that damage what you have built to succeed. You keep yourself from doing stupid things that cost you business."

The interest in etiquette is growing because of the reality of an international market, sophisticated competition, high expectations of customers, the emergence of women in positions of power, and the ethics crisis, for etiquette is based in ethics.

With etiquette, you will:

- Differentiate yourself in a competitive market.
- Interact skillfully with people of different backgrounds and varied interests who come from different parts of the country and world.
- Become comfortable and confident in the many settings required for conducting business. Etiquette enables you to put others at ease no matter what setting you are in. You feel good, too!
- Work well in the office. Etiquette updates and refines skills that enable employees to work better together.
- Handle awkward situations gracefully and rude people appropriately.
- Honor and sustain commitments to quality and excellence.

Remember, etiquette refines the way you do business. ■

Overcoming Shyness

Shyness can severely undermine you and your business. It can hinder your effectiveness, repel customers, and chase away career opportunities. When shy employees are reluctant to greet customers, customers perceive employees to be unfriendly or disinterested, not shy. When professional staff avoid attending or seem awkward at receptions because of shyness, others consider their behavior aloof, unrefined, even arrogant, not shy.

Jeff Akers, director of hospitality for a popular coastal resort, says, "In our business, we cannot afford for employees to be shy. Our job is to help our guests feel welcome and comfortable. We deliberately coach our staff to speak to our guests."

If you or your staff suffers from shyness, you can feel some relief to know many people — even accomplished professionals — wrestle with it. However, your self-consciousness can be misinterpreted. The following tips can help you overcome your shyness.

- **Take people one at a time.** When traveling for business, approach individuals rather than large groups. Speak to one person at a time when they approach your counter or pass you in the hall or parking lot.
- **Be helpful.** Often shy people are caring and sensitive and

Shy people who avoid attending or seem awkward at receptions, may appear aloof, unrefined, even arrogant.

worry about imposing themselves on others. However, people usually want to know you. Approach others. Doing so puts them at ease, making it easier for both to break the ice. Offer to help. Give good directions. Assume the host role at receptions, usher people around. Direct them to food and beverages and introduce them to others. If people enter your store, acknowledge them when they approach you. Consider approaching them first. Many people hide behind merchandise rather than speaking to customers.

• **Work to be impressed, not to impress.** Let others shine. When you think of making others feel important, you concentrate more on them and less on yourself. This usually reduces self-consciousness. Be the first to greet people. Smile. Introduce yourself.

• **A note to the outgoing.**

Shy people may run away from your outgoing manner. Some people who seem aloof could really be shy. Rather than overpower them, give shy people some room. If you sense people are shy, match the way they speak and move. Don't mock or mimic, but parallel their manner to move with them; be like them so that you become in tune with them.

Shyness plagues many accomplished professionals. With practice, you can control it and not have it control you. ∎

Recruiting New Members

Each year, many organizations kick-off membership drives. "Membership is the lifeblood of any organization to continue to grow and improve," says Julian Barton, membership chair of the South Carolina Society of Association Executives. "With more members, we can be more effective and serve our members."

However, the process of recruiting and sustaining members can be managed badly. Here are tips to refine how you handle newcomers.

• **Be deliberate about including new people.** Sounds simple, yet while old members extend a polite greeting, there can be subtle, even direct judgment, "Exactly, who are you and what do you bring?" I've witnessed what I call professional hazing in which new members are isolated, and the clique of old members remains impenetrable. Evaluate your entire system of recruitment. Do existing members talk only with each other? Can newcomers contribute quickly? They don't have to take the place by storm, but you might be able to use their talent.

• **Act glad to see newcomers.** Welcome them at the registration desk, not with a scripted greeting, but with genuineness. "Oh, yes, I have your name tag right here. Let me introduce you

To put people at ease and to get to know them quickly, discipline your introductions. Speak names slowly and distinctly.

to someone you might find interesting," or "Good to see you again," and say their name. Escort them around, maybe shifting them off to other members. Put guests at ease by pointing out officers and key members. A good way to make a bad impression is not to recognize someone you've met three times. Do what you can to remember names. Make notes if you must, even take pictures.

• **Be deliberate about introductions.** Yes, you can recognize newcomers just before lunch and highlight their names on the program. Yet to put people at ease and to get to know them quickly, discipline your introductions. Speak names slowly and distinctly. Add to the basics something complimentary or distinctive to make people feel special and to have enough information to start a conversation. Take your time. Aim for a few memorable visits. Go for quality, not quantity here.

• **Follow up with new or potential members.** We have all been carried away with hoopla, but service after the sale is important for credibility and membership retention. Check with new members periodically. Ask their observations and what else you can do to help them or improve your system. ■

Ann C. Humphries

Take Care With Names

Attempt to get people's names right! General Shalikashvili's (Sha-lee-KASH-va-lee, not so hard.) appointment as Chairman of the Joint Chiefs of Staff has called our attention to peoples' names and how we pronounce, spell, alter and accept them. So have the names of Rep. Marjolie Margolies-Mezvinsky (D.-Pa.); Colin Powell (Which is it 'COlin' or 'CAW-lin?'), Dr. Maya Angelou (It's 'Anja-LOW,' not 'AnjaLOO') the poet at President Clinton's Inauguration, Mike Krzyzewski (Sha-shev-ski), Duke's basketball coach, and scores of others.

In business, part of your success is due to how you manage the impressions you make, and silly, avoidable mistakes such as mispronouncing, misspelling, fearing, and laughing at people's names undermine you in a competitive world.

Gerald Worzywak (Wars-wak), manager of physician relations at Wake Medical Center in Raleigh, North Carolina, says, "I'll accept any number of pronunciations. I appreciate when people try."

Here are tips for managing names that might be unfamiliar to you.

•**Make an attempt.** Rather than try twice, then give up, and

Mistakes such as mispronouncing, fearing, and laughing at people's names undermine you in a competitive world.

assign a nickname, keep trying. People with unfamiliar names understand the difficulty their names pose for others. They are forgiving of sincere attempts, but they also recognize veiled ridicule and laziness. What impresses them are people and organizations who are familiar with and prepared for unusual names and, furthermore, people who take them in stride.

•**Practice until you get it right.** Especially when it is your job to introduce or recognize the individual, practice until you are comfortable. Your ease will project a message of acceptance and endorsement. Rather than say their name the way you think it should be said, say it closely to the way they say it.

•**Cue your co-workers.** When you encounter a person whose name is uncommon, spell it correctly and phonetically when you make their files, take their reservations, or relay their messages. Be deliberate when you introduce people. This way, you avoid the embarrassing, "We'll take you now, Mr. er...ah....HowDOYouPronounceYourName?" cavalier dismissals "Is it 'ShaKWEEL' or 'ShaKeil'?" or "Get a load of this one, everybody!"

When success is on the line, attention to details makes big differences. ∎

Preparing For Conventions (Part One)

Even with budget cuts, you may be required or need to attend a conference or convention. Convention costs are high whether you or your company underwrites your trip. To get the most for your time and money in attending state, regional, or national meetings, take time to prepare. You will find your travel and experience will be much smoother and profitable. Here are a few tips for being away.

• **Allow enough time to arrive.** You probably pry yourself from the office and race out of town to arrive at your destination tired and late. Instead, budget time to check in, freshen up, and attend the opening session. Usually, the opening program is a feature presentation, so don't cheat yourself.

• **Plan your outcome.** Outline what you want to accomplish. Review the program and focus on select topics. Commit to finding one important concept you can apply or relate back in the office. Map out the exhibits to plan your route, and save your feet. Budget for surprises, too. Allow yourself to consider something you never thought of.

Add personal benefits to your outcome — meeting nice peo-

Meet nice people and have a good time. This will prevent you from being too intense.

ple and having a good time. This will prevent you from being too intense.
- **Dress appropriately.** Dress professionally, even if you dress casually. Do not wear sweatsuits, shorts, T-shirts, and athletic shoes. And bring business cards! Position them where you can reach them easily without fumbling through your convention packet.
- **Plan to attend.** Even though you may be staying with friends in the city, prioritize your purpose: to visit your friends or to get the most from your meeting. If visiting, you may feel obligated to your hosts and skip important sessions.
- **Anticipate who will attend.** Refresh your memory about people you have met before. Rehearse questions to ask or topics to discuss. Remember and reference your last conversation with people. Make notes about people in your convention packet. Check off who you met and what you discussed. File for next year. ∎

Attending Conventions (Part Two)

Attending a conference can be overwhelming. To make the best of your trip, follow these tips while you attend.
• **Mingle.** Crowds of people can be overwhelming, but step right in. If you are alone, approach other people who are alone. Visit at the hors d'oeuvres table, reception desk, or on your way to or from activities, even in the restroom or on the elevator. Say something complimentary about anything, "Great band," "Good food," "Pretty city/hotel," "Moving program." Stand shoulder to shoulder with someone as you watch an event. Lean in and mention, "Lots of bright people," "Good point," even, "What do you think?" Then, introduce yourself. Say your name distinctly, so that people can understand you. Add your city, your line of work, or how many conventions you've attended.

If you are with friends or work associates, ask them to introduce you to people they know, and reciprocate. Don't band together. Split up for thirty minutes, then reconnect and trade notes on the people you met.

If the crowds at break time overwhelm you, go into the next

Talk with people, talk about lessons learned, issues you face, or problems you struggle with. Really communicate.

session and take a seat. Sherry Boecher, a management trainer from Overland Park, Kansas has a good icebreaker. She always takes two handouts, one to keep and one to share with someone she meets. Then she offers what she learned from the last session and asks what session you attended.

• **Circulate.** Plan to visit with people about five to ten minutes, then move on. If you both enjoy each other, great. Keep talking. Most people understand the need to circulate, so move on.

Avoid peppering people with questions without waiting for an answer. Avoid talking too much about yourself. Ask a respectable number of "How about you?" questions.

Remember, there are people who will interest you and those who won't, people with whom you agree, and others you won't, people who will be interested in you, and some who will ignore you. Filter the people and information to benefit you.

• **Pace yourself.** Exercise or take a nap. Eat and drink wisely. The sessions can be intense and the people stimulating. Afterwards, organize your notes. Throw out extraneous papers. Summarize, add numbers, and order the points you want to remember. Group business cards to remind you of whom you'll meet next time. Budget time to unpack and debrief. While the programs and people can be stimulating, the travel can be taxing. Budget time to rest. ■

The Rewards Of Patience

Have a little patience. We get in such a hurry in business, we forget the value patience can have for us. We become driven by tight deadlines, high expectations, and multiple projects, but patience can serve us well.

Rather than huffing at a customer who takes longer than usual to complete a form or answer a survey, give them time. Guide them through the process. Design your questions, so that they are easy to complete. Although you may complete the form multiple times a day, customers complete it only once.

Lynn Odom, office manager at Palmetto Utility Protection Service, Inc. in Columbia, South Carolina daily experiences the need for patience with customers. "We need to get good directions from our callers, but sometimes they are unable to describe the location well because they are in an unusual location, or they simply are unable to express themselves. We've learned to be more patient with callers, to guide them to give us information we need. This saves us time, helps us get the information we need, and leaves an impression that we are easy to deal with. That is valuable to us."

If someone has difficulty expressing themselves, don't rush to finish their sentences or talk for them. Pause. Wait, then

Patience is not to be perceived as neglect, passivity, or as reactive rather than proactive. It can be a strength.

suggest. You will show respect for them, which will serve you much better than impatience. If someone has difficulty completing a task, give them more room to work with, more support or more time. You may not have explained things well. Let people get acclimated to the job. You may have asked too much too soon. Hand things to people rather than throw or toss items. Wait, rather than force ideas, decisions, or sales that aren't right. Don't insult people because they take a little longer. Spend time doing things right rather than hurriedly and superficially completing them.

Patience is not to be perceived as neglect, passivity, or as reactive rather than proactive. It can be a strength. ∎

Beware A Hurried Manner

Beware a hurried manner. It can work against you in business.

Have you ever paused, then asked quizzically, "I beg your pardon?" when the person who answers the telephone races through the name of the company? If you've ever felt disregarded as you run down a corridor with someone to make a point, if you've had people finish your sentences, or cut short the discussion because they had other things to do, or if you've suffered the repercussions of an ill-thought strategy, then you know what I mean by a hurried manner.

Some people are consistently hurried. They rush here and there, appearing disorganized rather than important. You can hardly get an appointment or manage a conversation with them. When you do get a few precious moments, they arrive late and leave early. Your time with them is intense, directed, and rushed. Cordialities are few. The outcome leaves you shortchanged and short-tempered.

When the desk clerk processes your form in a rushed manner, you question the results. You feel like a number.

On the other hand there are people who demonstrate a calm steadiness about how they work. They are not to be rushed nor

> **Make sure you and your staff give adequate attention to issues, people, and processes. People will have more confidence in you.**

do they allow themselves to be. Each telephone call, each person, each situation gets appropriate attention.

Laura Wade, manager of Physician Services at Baptist Medical Center in Columbia, South Carolina, said, "I had a mentor who advised, 'Make a decision you can make again.' From that I learned, don't be impulsive. Think about the repercussions. Be thoughtful about the integrity of the decision. Could you duplicate it, especially in dealing with human resource issues?"

To be sure, there are certain times when your workload increases to hectic paces. The weekends may be frantic, or the holidays may strain your staff. There are even times when you must make quick decisions, however flawed.

Even when you are racing inside because there are so many things to do, resist being hurried. Make sure you and your staff give adequate attention to issues, people, and processes. People will respond to your confident manner and, therefore, have more confidence in you. ■

The Right Moves, Volume II

A Sharper Image

Dressing Down for Business

Casual days for business environments can be a disaster. With lean workforces who strain harder and harder to survive, organizations seek to increase motivation and show goodwill and appreciation by relaxing dress codes. Employees demand to be comfortable as an inexpensive concession for their toil.

But, let's be frank, casual days can be an embarrassing distraction.

Management usually means for you to wear respectable clothing even on casual days. That means a blazer or cardigan instead of a suit, flats instead of heels, tailored pants, not stretch pants, and flowing, looser fitting clothing, rather than knits that look like pajamas. It means clothing that looks updated and fresh and still covers your body substantially. It can even be a little trendy.

What it doesn't mean is bluejeans, warm-ups, athletic shoes, or clothing that is worn, out of shape, or ill-fitting. Nor does it mean for you to reveal your weekend persona or overtly display your sexuality.

Casual day is not an excuse to display poor taste, either. The rules which dictate a professional business appearance are also meant to disguise bad taste. Bob McGarvey, a writer in Venice,

Your gauge of appropriateness should be "Would clients, guests, or good management question my ability?"

California says, "Buying good clothes is a 'no brainer.' All you have to do is go to a respected store in town and let them pick it out for you. Why fight it? Casual clothes can be as hierarchical as traditional clothes." Bessie Simmons, an administrator in Charleston, South Carolina says, "Casual days are more trouble than they are worth. I've had to go out to buy clothes to wear on casual day."

Your gauge of appropriateness should be, "Would clients, guests, or good management question my ability? Will this be a distraction?"

You may argue, "But these professional clothes are uncomfortable." If they are, stop buying uncomfortable clothing. If your collar chokes you, your waistband pinches, or your jacket is restrictive, buy a different size. If you think your clothes are too expensive for the salary you draw, buy fewer pieces of better quality and change accessories.

Guidelines and approaches to casual days need to be as deliberate as the strategy for more traditional wear. ■

When The Heat Is On

It's July, and it's hot, but business continues. Appointments need to be met. You still need to drive, park, walk, deliver, and do many of the things you do all year, but now you must cope in weather topping 100 degrees and still maintain a professional demeanor.

Here are a few special tips.

• **Wear natural fibers.** Natural fibers are cooler. "Wool in a six-, seven-, or eight-ounce fabric is cooler than a polyester/wool blend," says Vaughn Granger, vice president of Granger-Owings, a men's specialty store in the southeastern United States. On hot days, wear suits and pants in tropical wools, cotton poplin, seersucker, or pincord fabrics and sport coats in linen, silk, wool, or natural fiber blends.

On the hottest days, wear 100 percent cotton shirts, "but do wear long sleeves," continues Granger. Short sleeve shirts with ties are not to be worn in business environments without a jacket. Wear all-cotton socks.

Linda Suber, corporate fashion director with Rackes, a women's specialty retailer points out, "Look as if you honor the importance of a professional appearance out of respect for the position you have and the people with whom you work. Look

The weather forces all business people to devise special strategies to maintain their health as well as their judgment in the heat.

at least as if you tried, but don't resort to casual summer wear. Never appear careless."
  • **Wear lighter colors.** Khaki, olive, taupe, and lighter grays and blues get you though heat waves easier. White shirts are cooler. Sport coats can work in the heat. They often are lighter in color and looser in weave.
  • **Wear looser fits and fewer layers.** Purchase clothing that has more room. Even in traditional fits, summer clothing in hot weather looks as professional in a slightly larger size and is more comfortable. Rather than work with your collar button undone to cope with the heat, buy neck collars with enough room to keep you cool. Wear suspender braces to give your waist room. Consider a suit or jacket that is unlined and on the hottest days, forego an undershirt.
  • **Keep your clothing pressed.** Tom Blackburn, a buyer with Lourie's, a specialty clothing retailer also located in a southern city, says, "Starched shirts seem to be hotter. Have your suits pressed rather than dry-cleaned with each wear. It's less expensive, and the clothing lasts longer."
  • **Maintain your grooming.** Avoid perfumes and colognes on hot days for they can easily sour. But use plenty of deodorant.
  With deliberate strategies, you'll survive the swelter. When the heat is on, you *can* keep your cool. ■

Hat Etiquette

Etiquette adapts to changing times, and through the years headgear has certainly changed. So let's talk about hats. You may think we don't wear hats much, but we do, lots of them — visors, baseball caps, cowboy hats, and sassy, summer straw hats.

Mini-battles erupt when children wear baseball caps to the table. In Columbia, South Carolina, Police Chief Charles P. Austin asks participants of indoor school assemblies to remove their hats. Elementary school principal, James L. Price, has a policy that children — girls and boys —cannot wear hats at school.

Let's explore today's hat etiquette.

• **Men, remove your hats when entering smaller spaces, homes, and more formal settings.** For example, you can wear your hat when you enter a lobby or corridor, but not when you enter a specific office or classroom. You can wear hats in fast food restaurants, but not in nice restaurants; in shopping malls, but not nice shops. You can wear hats in crowded, public elevators, but remove them in residential elevators. And, yes, remove hats for invocations, the Pledge of Allegiance, the National Anthem, and job interviews. Hats that accompany ethnic cos-

You may think we don't wear hats much, but we do — visors, baseball caps, cowboy hats, and sassy, summer straw hats.

tumes or religious practices remain on both in and out of doors.

Cindy Corwin of Leakey, Texas chuckles when she talks about western hat etiquette. "Around here, cowboys wear their hats so often, they have tans to their eyebrows. I even think restaurants raise the height of doors to be inviting." Hair creases are proudly nurtured as evidence of wearing hats.

Abe Cortez, owner of the World Famous Paris Hatters in San Antonio, Texas who customizes hats for European royalty and country and western stars says, "Wearing cowboy hats indoors is no problem when conducting western business or socializing in western settings. You wear your hat to a rodeo, a dance, barbecue restaurant, even country music awards, but those hats come off in more formal settings."

• **For women, you can wear a hat just about anytime unless it doesn't match your outfit, obstructs someone's view, or is prohibited as in schools.** You'd likely remove weather-related hats such as ski caps, visors, or hats that match your coat. Hats and turbans that match outfits for graduations, weddings, and worship, even shopping, stay on. ∎

The Sounds Of Business

Consider the sounds of conducting business — ringing cash registers, clicking keyboards, and chirping telephones. Then consider business noises that make people cringe, recoil, or fall down laughing in the employee lounge. Here are some of the most unpopular sounds of business and a big hint: "Don't do these."
- Drinking coffee, "Sluuurrrp.....Ahhhhh;"
- People unaware of how far their voices carry on airplanes, in lobbies, on pay phones and speaker phones;
- Yelling across the office when you should go to people or wait until they return;
- Loud, personal conversations at front desks and kitchens in restaurants and hotels;
- Clanking silver during eating and cleanup;
- Smacking and finger licking;
- Door slamming and loud talking in hotel corridors late night and early morning;
- The overbearing clop of shoes which indicate, "I have important business. Don't you?"
- Public fingernail clipping;
- Gum snapping and popping;

The Right Moves, Volume II

Take a quiet minute to reflect on the sounds of conducting business. How do you sound?

• "Psst" to someone who is already on the phone;
• Continuous sniffing, rather than blowing a runny nose, and the ever popular "Hrrawk" of throat clearing;
• Fingernail flicking, pencil tapping, fist or finger pounding, coin jingling, and key rattling;
• Talking during the Pledge of Allegiance;
• Loud sighs and yawns, booming sneezes;
• Unwrapping cellophane candy during concerts.

(Shhhh!) Take a quiet minute to reflect on the sounds of conducting business. Now, take a quiet moment and think, "How do I sound?" ■

The Right Moves, Volume II

A Way With Words

A Way With Words

Want to reduce problems with difficult people? Eliminate common phrases people consider rude and abrupt, and you'll find people will respond to you and your business much more positively.

The first of the phrases is, "Our company policy states," and its variations such as, "You are required," "That's against our policy," or "You can't do that." When hearing these phrases, people escalate to irrational and loud behavior, and your problems explode, especially when your staff uses a taunting or robot-voice tone.

Change your reaction. Rephrase your responses to issues of what you *can* do. Offer options. Express concern. "What we can do is," "Why don't you try…," "Oh, I'm sorry about this. I know it's an inconvenience. Let's see what we can do to expedite this."

Another abrupt word in business is "but." Think of your reaction to someone who says, "You are doing a great job, but," or "That's a great idea, but." You sense the reverse. You anticipate the bad news. To soften this and accomplish your purpose, say, "You are doing a good job, and," or "That's a great job; however." The words "and" and "how-

Eliminate corporate speak people consider rude; you'll find people respond to you and your business more positively.

ever" ease the transition and keep you from becoming pedantic.

Lastly, eliminate what I call sniffing phrases, "He's not in," "She's in a meeting," or "He's on vacation." Offer clarification or helpfulness, "I expect him back after four," or "She should be out by 11:30, would you like to speak to Barbara?"

A way with words does help you in business. ■

Ann C. Humphries

Grammar And Pronunciation

Grammar! Pronunciation! They are required especially in the service industry or when talking to the public, but oh, the misuse and abuse of the language. Dismissing or ignoring how you speak or how your employees sound to others is folly. If you sound uncertain, ignorant, or pretentious, you undervalue the credentials you have. You risk losing your client base and the respect of the people you serve. Your work will be harder to accomplish. Even with the diversity of the work environment, deliberate business communication skills are critical.

Although language adapts to different situations, the business world is formal, even in casual environments. Therefore, business language becomes more formal. When you master the language, your work becomes easier to perform. Promotions are easier to achieve, and arguments easier to make. You have an edge. The ability to shift your language to adapt to the group you are with is invaluable.

Some grammatical errors are overlooked, but others grate and are considered serious. They invite snickers. When people hear consistent misuse of the language, they begin to question the user's other skills and judgments. Here are some of the most irritating errors in grammar that undermine your reputa-

> **If you sound uncertain, ignorant, or pretentious, you undervalue the credentials you have. You risk losing your client base.**

tion.
- "Where is it at?" should be "Where is it?" Lose the "at."
- "Send it to him and I" might seem more formal, but it is wrong. "Bring it to him and me" is correct.
- "She don't" should be "She doesn't."
- "Y'all didn't did it yet," should be "Y'all didn't do/haven't done it yet."
- "Me and him are going," should be "He and I are going."

Common mispronunciations are:
- "pacifically" for "specifically,"
- "Often" should be pronounced "Offen."
- "Hisself" should be "himself." "Theirself" should be "themselves."
- "Irregardless" should be "regardless."

Recognize the difference between accents, dialect, grammar, and mispronunciations. Accents can be wonderful. With development, they can be exciting and interesting; however, uncontrolled, exaggerated accents can be a limitation. Think of your perceptions of accents from Boston, upper Michigan, the South Carolina Lowcountry, or Appalachian mountains.

Listeners, broaden your standards. The business world is more diverse. Speakers, become aware of how you sound and, as a result, how you are perceived. ■

Telephone Skills

So, you think you know how to use the telephone? If you do, then you can avoid many problems. Good telephone manners and skills are an asset. Here's a little brush up on telephone skills to avoid what appears to be unprofessional behavior.

People consider the following telephone behaviors to be rude.

1. Not identifying yourself when you call or when you answer. Say your name and company or department distinctly when you receive a call. Stop rushing. When you place a call, say who you are and why you are calling.

2. Long, unattended holds. Being put on hold abruptly is something people do not like. Get back to people within thirty seconds, then return every minute or two. Offer to take a message.

3. Unpleasant voice. A lack of warmth, a screening tone, and being short can offend people. Avoid effecting a "robot voice," i.e., answering the phone the same way, everyday, with a machine-like quality. Also in this category are people who ask your name, then tell you your party is not in. "You feel as if people learn who you are, then choose not to talk once they know it is you," writes one reader.

Also offensive are people who use voice mail exclusively, do not return phone calls, or who use offensive language.

Other telephone skills to practice include returning calls and simply being a good listener.

People appreciate the following telephone behaviors. Practice the following techniques so your telephone skills will reflect a professional image.

1. Develop a good voice and vocabulary. Surveys reveal that people enjoy the following telephone behaviors: saying "Please" and "Thank you," having a pleasant voice, a voice with a smile and personality, and a positive attitude.

2. Take complete messages. Many people consider answering the phone to be a chore and are unwilling to take messages. Offer to take a message and include the basics of date, time, and correct number. Sign the message. If people have questions, they can call you. Let people know a good time to reach their party.

3. Transfer calls well. This essential task is often botched, yet it is one of the details that projects exceptional professionalism. Tell your party you are transferring them. Let the person on the other end know who is calling and what they want. Then, when the two parties are connected, the person answering can say, "Yes, Ann. Steve told me you wanted to talk about..."

Other telephone skills to practice include returning calls promptly, helping people reach someone who could help them, and simply being a good listener. Practice these techniques and upgrade your skills and image. ∎

Effective Presentations

If your position or interests require you to make presentations, be deliberate about rehearsing your remarks. The risks you take with incomplete preparation are too great, even for routine meetings. You cannot always charm audiences with your earnestness, enthusiasm, or track record. Amateur public speaking by people in positions who should know better leaves audiences doubting the speakers' abilities and judgment of their employers.

If you are faced with a presentation for an upcoming event, consider these tips to protect your image and that of your organization.

• **Respect the event.** Audiences do not always accept impromptu remarks, especially when they should have been prepared. If you remain tense about your presentations, you'll likely discipline yourself to prepare well. A rule of thumb states that speeches take six to eight hours preparation for every hour delivered.

• **Decide on the impressions you want to make.** Answer an important question — "What outcomes do I want?" What you decide is not as important as *that* you decide. Examples include,

The risks you take with incomplete preparation are too great. You can't always charm audiences.

"Motivate the organization to change," "Generate enthusiasm for these ideas," "Have them consider us innovators," "Get three leads," or "Have them like me."

•**Determine your themes.** To accomplish your outcome, focus on one to three themes and reiterate them. You won't appear simplistic. The audience will appreciate and respect the fact that your remarks have continuity. Interweave your themes throughout your content.

•**Take charge.** All eyes will be on you as you take your place, so move with confidence. Adjust your clothing and clear your throat before you rise. As you take your position, pause, take time to look at the audience, then begin. With this brief silence, you will capture people's attention, signal your beginning and subtly indicate your remarks are worthy of their attention. Too many people rush this part. Also, test the microphone before you speak, adjusting it to ensure it captures your voice.

With careful attention to a few details, your speeches and presentations will work *for*, not against you. ∎

Ann C. Humphries

Telling Jokes Is No Joke

Joke-telling is serious business. Amateurs probably need to leave it to the professionals. Otherwise, they and the organizations they represent look stupid.

Who doesn't like a good joke to loosen up the crowd, ease the tension, or build good will? We all admire and appreciate a good joke and joke teller. In fact, the best joke tellers and comedy writers make megabucks.

Lately, we have seen public joke-telling backfire. Tellers become caught in their own traps of overt racial, religious, and sexual discrimination not to mention blatant tastelessness. The squirming itself becomes comical as the teller scrapes together a weak defense while retreating. Worse still is when they innocently wonder, "What went wrong?" or show a shocking lack of contrition.

Nicholas Gibler who owns a translating company in Monterrey, N.L., Mexico asks that American executives tell him ahead of time the jokes they plan to tell, "So I can adjust the joke for it to be well received by the audience. That's the intent of the joke anyway."

Think about the public reaction to the limp-wristed, lisped responses of Governor Doug Wilder of Virginia and Colonel

If someone tells a joke you find offensive, call it to their attention. Sitting there stone-faced or tittering with them is not enough.

Oliver North to media questions. Take, for example, local civic clubs which try to recruit women and minorities to build membership, but which continue to open meetings with jokes in ethnic dialects or which ridicule wives.

In a *USA Today* article, comedian David Brenner says, "Don't do anything that's hurtful. Don't make fun of the underdog, ever." *Tonight Show* host Jay Leno says the only thing over the line is, "loss of human life." David Koresh jokes were funny until the explosion. If you poke fun at one group, poke fun at all of them.

If someone tells a joke you find offensive, call it to their attention. Sitting there stone-faced or tittering with them is not enough. Interrupt. Boo. Spread the word. Write a formal complaint.

Joke. Laugh. But rethink the jokes you tell in public. Tell the appropriate ones, but don't tell or allow hurtful joke-telling especially in business settings. ■

Risk Telling the Truth

Tell the truth. Always tell the truth.

Well, the truth is that *truth* requires clarity, courage and a strategy for how to tell it.

In business, the truth can be so unexpected and uncommon that it brings freshness and power to the workplace. Business people are desperate for the truth. We need to hear, "The system isn't working," "This person cannot deliver," "I feel uncomfortable," even, "Yes, you do seem to have put on a few pounds."

The truth can be a relief. If you've received a diagnosis, even if it is bad, at least you can work with what you know. When someone finally says what needs to be said, you feel the pressure drop. When the news finally comes, you stop spending energy on wondering, "What next?"

Truth is also a motivator. Think of your reaction to someone who recognizes the reality of a situation and begins to solve the problem. Imagine the response of employees when administration celebrates their contributions to a difficult task. Remember how energized you are when you see the pureness of an issue.

Realizing the truth is important. So is how you tell it. It can slip out by mistake with people sputtering and over explaining. It can require anger, tears, and shouts to get people's attention.

As you determine how to tell the truth, consider your outcomes. The truth can embarrass, anger, and elevate you.

It can overpower an issue if hurled with brute force. Then, when given with humor and a light touch, it can enable people to get the point and save face.

As you determine how to tell the truth, consider your outcomes. The truth can embarrass, anger, and elevate you. Anticipate the repercussions. Prepare to defend yourself. Be willing to withstand the risks. It may be worth it.

Risk telling the truth in business and practice defining it. As well, consider your intent and its reception. You'll find truth's presence can be refreshing. ∎

Ann C. Humphries

An Encouraging Word

Take advantage of every opportunity to encourage people. In the rush to accomplish and the race to achieve, business people work hard to get results. Without encouragement, people second-guess their contributions, let doubt overpower, and tend to drift. Employees can only go so far on their own initiative. Even with successes under their belt, they still need encouragement, albeit a different kind, to stay the course and achieve results, for criticism is everywhere. Encouragement is a motivator. It is not a weakness. It isn't coddling, and people do not expect more money as a result of it.

In the business world, we're all treading new ground and making some rules as we go. In stressful times, people need encouragement and feedback. They also need it in the small, but steady progress made everyday. So often, we assume people are aware of our support, so we don't call, fax, or jot a note; but a lack of response can easily be interpreted as indifference or disagreement.

Lorraine Plaxico, a new manufacturer's sales representative in Columbia, South Carolina, thought she was doing well, heard indirectly through the secretary and her associates that her manager was pleased, but remained uncomfortable and

Opportunities for encouragement come delicately. Be ready with a range of responses. Your business and reputation will grow.

uncertain until she and her manager met to discuss work. "Then, I heard it straight from him. He was specific, proud, almost effusive and, frankly, I needed to hear it," she said. "We are on the road so much," she continues, "We communicate through voice mail and faxes and are always in a hurry; but simple, straightforward praise sure goes a long way."

In contrast was another manager Plaxico knew of who was always citing money problems, quoting sales figures, emphasizing competition, and harping on the negative. "He didn't get the results he could have and blamed it on employee morale. He missed several opportunities to compliment his staff which would have inspired them to their goal."

Sometimes encouragement is forthcoming from others, but sometimes you have to ask for it. Insist that people tell you how you are doing, that they are proud of you, that you are leading, accomplishing, and producing. During turbulent times, you don't need to solicit the critics. Sure, listen to them, but build your strength with supporters for the tasks ahead. Support your staff when they are developing new programs. Give them room. Protect and encourage them.

Opportunities for encouragement come delicately. They can be subtle, and they can be direct. Be ready with a range of responses, and your business and reputation will grow. ■

Proposal Strategies

As you watch business leaders and politicians present their ideas, you become aware of deliberate tactics involved in making their proposals appealing. Some of these strategies can help you in your office or on your quality team. If you have a great idea, here are tips for presenting it well.

- **Determine what you want.** Be honest about what you seek to accomplish. Do you want your idea implemented because it saves money or simplifies work? Are you seeking a foothold, recognition, an alliance, or a new identity? If you consider all your preferred outcomes, you'll likely focus to get what you want. However, have alternative plans, so that you can accomplish something.
- **Make it easy for people to accept.** Think through what you propose. How would it appeal to you? Make your proposal straightforward and clear. Act with confidence. Do not ramble in either written or oral presentations. Lead people through your reasoning. Include an outline, even pictures, graphs, or documentation. Highlight benefits.
- **Anticipate questions and answer them before they are asked.** Acknowledge problems with your ideas and offer your recommendations for solutions.

Make your proposal straightforward and clear, and act confident.

- **Consider your timing.** You might want to introduce your idea first, then return with a more thorough plan. Ask the committee leader to include you on the agenda. Surprising people is rarely effective.
- **Involve people.** Develop a team approach rather than an individual one. Present your ideas informally to people whose opinions you respect. Adjust your strategy to incorporate the suggestions you like. Consider presenting your proposal to people who will most likely resist you. If you can get their involvement and contributions early, they may be less likely to undermine you later. You may also discover why they disagree which will help prepare your defense.
- **Realize not all your ideas will be accepted.** Usually a fraction of proposals survive, so don't brood. Let some ideas go. For ideas important to you, persevere. Look for ways to reintroduce them with a fresh approach. ∎

Ann C. Humphries

Advising Management of Changes

Some managers tell people what to do rather than listening to ideas from employees. When management continues dictating policy to employees without involving them and soliciting their opinions, employee productivity goes down. Employees often have ideas on how to improve operations but lack the skills and confidence to introduce their ideas to management.

Here are suggestions for employees who want to introduce changes.

• **Consider that you are all on the same team.** Stop engaging in the "us" versus "them" polarization.

• **To clarify your issues, write them down.** They look different in black and white. Include solutions you recommend, benefits to the organization, resources needed for implementation, and expected results. Consider getting a team involved, but go it alone if you must. Also, be clear about what you want to have happen.

Order your list from management's perspective and blend it with organization goals, adding phases and emphasizing results. Anticipate resistance and prepare your response to it. In

Order your list from management's perspective and blend it with organization goals, adding phases and emphasizing results.

your meeting, provide handouts or an agenda that is easy to follow. Smart management will respect thoughtful, organized presentations.

One result may be, "We can't do that." Have enough options so that you get, "What we can do is....."

Above all focus on what is possible. The economy puts many companies in tumult, so make your suggestions easy to implement and look for ways to team up with your organization. ■

The Right Moves, Volume II

Social Graces For Business Places

Company Party Manners

You know it's coming. You'll do anything to avoid it. It's too much trouble, and it's only for show. What is it? The office party, where you're expected to make an appearance, pretend to have a good time with people you don't know or necessarily even like in an atmosphere where conversations range from monosyllabic responses to gay superficiality.

But, hey, this is business, and you have to attend. If you don't, you risk being labeled haughty, inaccessible, or a poor team player — unflattering labels for today's business world.

Whether you're a vice president invited to every night-shift party, the spouse who never interacts with company employees, or if you are just painfully shy, looking as if you are enjoying yourself at required company functions is an unstated part of your job.

Robin D. moved with her husband to Tennessee for his work, and they were both invited to a company party. "You sort of have to go, and it was deadly. We were sitting at the table chewing in silence. It was the longest evening."

To avoid awkward moments like these, here are a few tips to help you relax and turn a gloomy moment into an enjoyable, productive outing.

Don't hide at parties. Introduce yourself and make a positive comment about something in which others are involved.

•**Rehearse the party.** Anticipate people you will meet and practice what to ask them. Sounds simple, but across the room, you see the VIP guest, the Big Wig, Head Honcho, even the mayor. Instead of ducking behind the potted plant, plan to introduce yourself and make a positive comment about something in which they are involved. Your interaction might last fifteen seconds, but your good will remains all year. Do this even if you are the spouse or guest. Ask whomever you accompany to let you know who will be there and what you might discuss with them. You'll make them look great!

Approach these required events as if they could be fun. Parties are intended to be a celebration. They are given in your honor, not as an obligation or chore. Feel pleased to be included, and you will relax. ∎

Holiday Formalities

During the holidays, people have opportunities to perpetuate good will and celebrate. Yet out in public and under the influence of holiday festivities, people can do the most ridiculous things, undermining their professional credibility.

When people are prepared and confident in public settings, they solidify their professional reputation.

To prepare you for traps; to give you an edge, here is ETICON's Annual List of Holiday Do's and Don'ts.

•*Do* **RSVP**. Let people know your plans. Start by thanking them for including you, tell them whether you can accept and end with praise, "Thank you for inviting me to the reception. I'm sorry I'm unable to come; I know I will miss a great party."

Do not say, "I'm calling for _____ (your boss). She's unable to attend." Do not waffle… "I will try to come," or "He's unsure of his plans." Do not be a "no-show." If you can't attend, let them know as soon as possible. If you said you would come but don't, call the next day to apologize.

•*Do* **dress appropriately**. Wear dark suits and dressier fabrics in the evening. Even if you are invited to a drop-in after work, modify your standard attire by wearing nicer jewelry, a dressier blouse or holiday shoes. For men, wear a dark suit, then change

People who are poised, prepared and confident in public settings solidify their professional reputation.

to a fresh, spread collar shirt and dressier tie. If the event is casual, make sure your casual clothes sustain your business image.

• *Do not* wear tweeds or light-colored suits to an evening reception, definitely not to a black tie event. Watch the blinking reindeer and jingle bells on holiday sweat suits at business parties. A silly image at parties can carry over to business.

• *Do* **arrive on time at concerts.** If you anticipate leaving early, get aisle seats so you can leave discreetly. Bring mints for throat tickles or excuse yourself if you find yourself coughing excessively or blowing your nose.

• *Do not* whisper, bring candy in crinkly cellophane or leave mid-way during a performance.

• *Do* **write thank you notes...** to hosts of receptions, for dinner in someone's home, even to suppliers for holiday gifts over eight dollars. Do not write a canned, insincere note. ∎

Here's A Toast

The time for a celebration is any time as long as an appropriate event is taking place. Many events occur throughout the year — graduations, engagements, weddings, retirements, and awards banquets. Toasting, frequently a part of most celebrations, can send shy people into shivers and overbearing people into boring harangues. To help you feel more at ease when proposing a toast, here are a few tips.

- **Prepare.** Where is a good toast when you need it? Just when you need a toast, your mind goes blank. To overcome this dilemma, carry an all-purpose toast in your wallet, so that you don't drone, "Here's mud in your eye." And don't forget to rehearse.
- **Orchestrate toasts.** Planned toasts launch the festivities and pave the way for spontaneous toasts. Enlist friends to help you get the attention of the crowd. Alert the food serving staff, so they will be quiet or absent when you begin. Limit the time allotted for toasts by saying, "We have time for one more," when it's necessary to bring toasting to a close.

As a guest, coordinate toasts with hosts to avoid upstaging them. Also, beverages poured at dessert time may be intended for toasting, so don't gulp the drinks.

Keep it simple, sincere, and short. Giving a toast is no time for climbing onto soap boxes.

- **Keep it simple, sincere, and short.** Giving a toast is no time for climbing onto soap boxes. Be kind, complimentary, and brief, around one minute or less, and look the honoree in the eye as you begin to drink.
- **Speak up.** When you begin your toast, rise, lift your glass, and speak in a slightly louder voice.
- **Watch your posture.** Both men and women may rise to honor a dignitary. In small groups, you may remain seated, but straighten your posture.
- **Be a gracious recipient.** If you are being honored by a toast, thank the person who raised the toast. Drink only after everyone else does; otherwise you appear to be toasting yourself. If, however, the "toaster" seems to be waiting on you, lift your glass with a hearty, "Thank you," waiting momentarily for them to drink. Then, follow.
- **Toast anytime.** No need to wait for a formal celebration with wine or champagne. You can toast on the beach with soft drinks or in a restaurant quietly with friends. A few guidelines and a little preparation pave the way for smooth, effective, fun toasts and celebrations. ■

Table Manners

The business world offers you many opportunities to eat in public. Whether you attend an awards banquet or eat with clients or business associates, review your table manners to feel comfortable and confident.

• **Which items are yours?** A meeting planner lamented that because she attends to last-minute details, she often arrives after the meal has begun to find her bread plate, glasses, napkin, and coffee cup being used by others. Some simple cues can help you remember what belongs to you at the table setting. Items with four letters go on your left (Left has four letters.) FORK and FOOD are on the L-E-F-T. That means your bread plate is on your left. Spoons, knives, and drinks are on the right (five letters) — SPOON, KNIFE, and DRINK.

• **When do I begin?** When at a table of eight or ten, wait until four people are served to begin to eat. If you have not been served, be gracious and encourage those served to begin. You need not stare nor look forlorn. In smaller groups where there is a definite host, wait to eat until the host begins or invites you to start.

• **Start the process.** After people are settled, reach for the

Being sure of your table etiquette will make you comfortable and confident wherever you're dining.

items closest to you and begin to circulate them. Offer the rolls to the person to your left. Hold the basket for them, take one yourself, then pass to the right. Follow the same procedure for the sugar, butter, and salt and pepper. Pass cream and salad dressings with the handle toward the person receiving the item.

•**Welcome arrivals.** Introduce yourself and others. When people join you, nod, smile, and pull out their chairs. Men can make a half-rise attempt. Women can straighten their posture as a greeting. During the meal, be deliberate about including people around you in the conversation. Avoid "playing up" to the dominant person.

If you want to circulate at the banquet, greet people quickly, say a few sentences, then move on. Do not hover over their table.

•During the meal presentation, keep toothpicks out of your mouth, avoid running your tongue over your teeth, tugging at your belt, and crunching ice.

A business meal is a public forum requiring basic attention to table manners. Practice so you represent your organization well. ∎

Holiday Etiquette — Part One

The holiday season—No doubt, you'll receive invitations to events you wish you could avoid, but which require your attendance. You are never comfortable in these settings and even dismiss their purpose and importance. Yet, these events can reveal a lot about you and the organization you represent.

Carl Crist, an engineer with Winn Dixie in Jacksonville, Florida says, "These events are often perceived to be political. People don't want to, but they have to go for corporate reasons. It gets even harder when spouses say, 'I went last year. You're on your own this time.' You really need strategies to get through these events."

To turn holiday business receptions into successes, here are a few techniques.

• **Decide to have a good time.** Simple idea. If you approach these events rigid and tense, you will probably have a bad experience. Instead, relax a little. Rather than become overwhelmed by the crowds, create reasonable goals such as, "Meet three new people and speak to Tony, Darlene, and Ms. Faberatti."

On the other hand, treat these as business events, not personal social parties. Maintain some restraint and formality.

During the holidays, being "rough around the edges" may be too costly in these days of downsizing or tough competition.

- **Dress appropriately.** People can be inappropriately casual, conservative, or cavalier at these events. Dressing too casually comes across as arrogant or "out-of-it." Change shirts and ties; freshen makeup and change jewelry to give the event the honor it deserves.

  Resist the spandex or silly cummerbunds. If you are unsure about appropriate attire, ask the host.

- **RSVP.** Soon after you receive your invitation, respond to let your hosts know if you are coming or not. This is an area which can polish or dull your professional reputation. An "I'll try to," is unacceptable, even haughty. Always thank people for inviting you, then be decisive, "I'm unable to come because of prior commitments," or "I look forward to coming."

Whether you like it or not, your social skills or lack thereof represent the breadth and depth of your business acumen. Being "rough around the edges" may be too costly in these days of downsizing or tough competition. Take some time to prepare to influence your success. ■

Holiday Etiquette — Part Two

Attending holiday receptions can be a fun or dreaded event, even a little of both. To be comfortable at events often required for business, follow these simple strategies.

• **Anticipate who will be there.** Many business receptions are repeat events with familiar people you can count on seeing. To be most at ease, visualize who will be there, "Let's see, Vince and Sybil will be there, the Chows, and the new person, Mr. Guiterrez from Fort Worth." Next, plan what you might discuss with them. This may seem to be a lot of trouble, but the rehearsal can smooth conversation which otherwise may be awkward with people you see less often. It also prevents the panic that can set in when you've forgotten the name of someone you should know.

Don't forget to prepare your guests, too. Command performances can be frightening for people unfamiliar with your group. Tell your guests whom they're likely to meet. They'll appreciate the favor.

• **Arrive and leave on time.** Lucky you! You may have several events the same evening. If you are rushing, remember the *thirty-thirty-thirty* rule. Stay at least thirty minutes, arrive within thirty minutes of the time the event begins, and leave no later

Prepare your guests. Command performances can be frightening for people unfamiliar with your group.

than thirty minutes after it is supposed to end. To get away from talkative people, simply say, "Excuse me. I'd like to speak to Pat before she leaves. So nice to talk with you," or "Great to see you. Have a good holiday," or "Why don't we refill our plates?" and get them moving.

•**Introduce yourself and others.** Wear your name tag high on your shoulder, print your name so that it can be read at a distance of three feet, and be quick to offer your hand and say who you are. Occasionally you will introduce yourself to someone you have met, but most everyone appreciates people who take them off the spot by introducing themselves. Introduce others around you, too. If you can't remember a name, admit it quickly or stall for time by saying what you do remember, "Good to see you. The last time we saw each other was in Orlando. You had just returned from your vacation, I think."

Social graces in business places can pay off. ■

Flying The Red, White, And Blue

When patriotic times of the year roll around, it's great to have "flag" etiquette well in hand. Traditionally, Flag Day, Memorial Day, Independence Day, and President's Day represent ideal times to fly the red, white, and blue, but anytime is a great time to show your patriotism.

Many of us were taught in school how to respect the flag, but a lot of time may have passed since we learned how to show that respect. Not everyone has served in the military either, where respect for the flag is absolute. Whether you celebrate the holidays, attend meetings or sporting events, here are simple, updated techniques for honoring our country and the symbols that represent it.

• **According to formal etiquette, the flag should not be a part of clothing, home decoration, or disposable items.** Too bad commercial distributors don't respect this bit of etiquette. I just received a catalog with napkins, trays, T-shirts, even inner tubes festooned with the flag. I've even seen barbecue served on flag paper plates.

Although the flag code prohibits the commercial use of the flag, it is one of those interpretations that is overlooked. George Cahill of the National Flag Foundation in Pittsburgh says, "Just

According to formal etiquette, the flag should not be a part of clothing, home decoration, or disposable items.

as the world has changed, so has the manner in which we use flags and flag impressions. Look at the flag stamp. That's disposable." Like etiquette, rules and customs change, and the more you work with them, the more you realize what matters and what doesn't.

"On the positive side, the flag is much more everyone's flag than it was fifty years ago," Cahill continues. "The most important thing is that you get out the flag and fly it....frequently. Keep it clean, dry, and in good repair and proudly explain why the flag, as a symbol of our nation, is worthy of respect."

- **Whenever the national anthem is played, rise and sing.** When the Pledge of Allegiance is given, stop and show your attention — no eating, smoking, or talking. Pause if you're on your way to your seat. Sing the anthem or recite the pledge or at least attempt to. Place your right hand over your heart which is the civilian salute. Turn to the flag. If the flag is absent during the anthem, turn toward the music. Men remove their hats — including baseball and cowboy hats — and place them at the left shoulder. Non-US citizens should rise and be quiet, but need not sing, say the words, or salute.

Showing respect for the symbols that represent our country is important. A little review improves your confidence, especially in public settings. ■

The Business Art of Gift-Giving

You probably won't agonize over what gifts to send business associates (Who has time for that?), but you might look sloppy and mechanical or miss an opportunity to build good will by doing it wrong. Here are tips on business gift-giving.

• **Be clear of your purpose.** Do you want to show appreciation for business or curry favor; honor hard work or give out of obligation; make someone feel special or be dazzling yourself? Clarify your purpose to keep your gifts appropriate. When you admit your gag gift is indeed mean-spirited, you might want to reconsider.

• **You do not have to give gifts.** Business has been tight for some time now, so to get what might be a more effective impact, for fewer dollars, consider writing a special note on a holiday card. Do not worry about not having a gift for someone who surprises you with one. An opportunity to reciprocate later will surely arise.

Bosses rarely expect gifts, either. If you want to honor them, send something inexpensive and impersonal like food or flowers, not anything that looks as if you are seeking favor. Ask a trusted friend, "How would this look?" and ask yourself, "Could I defend this?" However, for lower paid staff who

> **Don't worry about not having a gift for someone who surprises you with one. A chance to reciprocate later will surely come up.**

perform personal services or dirty work, a small gift certificate acknowledges their year-round contributions.

• **Present gifts well.** Pretty wrapping can make inexpensive gifts look nice. Use gift tags, not your business card. Exchange gifts with personal office friends privately.

• **Be careful with holiday cards and greetings.** Surprise! Many business people do not celebrate Christmas, and they tire of your imposing your brand of faith on them. You are safer to send "Season's Greetings" or wish people "Happy Holidays" in business settings. When you send cards, add a special note. To only sign your name and enclose your business card is impersonal and over solicitous.

• **If you must refuse a gift, do so graciously.** Send a note with the gift saying that you appreciate the gesture, but you are unable to accept. Then, do not discuss the gift again. If you get something you don't want or need, donate it to charity.

• **Write thank you notes.** Even when gifts are given to show appreciation, a sincere thank you note is in order. ∎

Thank You Notes

Thank you notes are a joy to receive but a bother to write. They're confusing as to whom should receive them and when and why to send them. Your subconscious nags you until you write them. And you're annoyed when you don't receive them.

Here are a few tips on writing thank you notes.

- **You can still write thank you notes for the holiday gifts you received.** Premier thank you notes are written within two or three days of receiving a gift, but, frankly, givers welcome acknowledgement any time.
- **Send thank you notes for almost all your gifts.** Writing notes keeps you from over-expressing yourself to the point of sounding insincere or guilty. Jot a note to coworkers who surprised you with a thoughtful remembrance, neighbors who might have dropped a basket of fruit at your doorstep, even to vendors who sent you holiday packages as thanks for the year's business. You can thank close friends or associates in person or over the phone, but do take the extra step to write when they do something special or go to extra trouble.
- **Send thank you notes when you have been a guest in someone's home for dinner, a party, or overnight.** You need not send them to people you see regularly or to family, but

Thank you notes have a long shelf life for a nominal investment and simply make good business sense.

thank you notes are nice every once in a while even to that group.

•Use small business stationery for business thank you notes. Have nice personal stationery for gifts and gestures that are more personal, even though they are for business. You can type them, but resist standardizing them. We all recognize form letters. When a formal approach would be overkill, look for clever greeting cards to express light-hearted thanks.

•Use stamps, not metered postage. Place them carefully on someone's desk. If you must, send them through the interoffice mail, but avoid handing someone a thank you note. Thank you notes by electronic mail are better than nothing but remain a secondary solution.

Good thank you notes are uncommon. More often, they have a hurried, mechanical feel; yet, even busy, prominent people take time for personal notes of thanks. They know thank you notes have a long shelf life for a nominal investment. They simply make good business sense. ∎

The Right Moves, Volume II

Dealing With Differences

Ann C. Humphries

Gender Etiquette in the Workplace

The Tailhook scandal and the Clarence Thomas/Anita Hill face-off focused our attention on issues of gender in the workplace.

A recent survey revealed uncomfortable workplace behaviors that detract from the ability to work professionally.

Predominant issues raised were how often business men and women refer to how women appear, rather than how they perform. Personal comments, albeit innocent ones, can strike a nerve because for so long women's worth has been based on how they look rather than how they work.

Related to this issue is the frequent question women are asked, "What does your husband do?" or "Who takes care of your children?" This is sensitive, too, for men are rarely asked similar questions, and historically, a woman's value was linked to the man she was with. If you get a reaction from a woman when you compliment her looks or ask about her husband or children without even introductory conversation, this is why.

Another comment mentioned often includes assuming and assigning women to perform certain roles beyond getting the coffee. The subtleties of women feeling separated by gender include consistently being asked to take the minutes, get the copies, arrange for the children, answer the phone, even bring

Women often feel "talked down to" when they have their concerns disregarded as emotional.

the desserts and salads when men just pick up the chicken. It also includes not being assigned work due to childcare arrangements.

Women often feel "talked down to" when they have their concerns disregarded as emotional, "that time of the month," or just a "cat fight." Their conversations are interrupted or rephrased. More often, they are called by their first names when men are referred to by title; they are greeted by backrubs and weak handshakes and referred to as "girls," "honey," or "my daughter." Also listed were dirty jokes told in public or private in the workplace, put downs of wives in jokes, or snickering when profanity is used, "Oh, I forgot. There is a lady present."

Workplace behaviors that enable you to work professionally include giving women equal assignments of work regardless of gender, no sexual overtones, genuine friendliness, businesslike conversations, inclusive spoken and written language, and acceptance that women should be included, no question, no explanation needed, no fights. ■

Ann C. Humphries

Religious Diversity

Religion creeps into business whether it is supposed to or not. Sometimes its presence is innocuous, and other times it is oppressive.

As the American workforce becomes more diverse, religious diversity will emerge more often as a business issue.

To accommodate individual preferences for worship and to avoid insensitivity, however subtle or bold, follow these etiquette concepts. By doing so, people are able to follow their own religious paths, allowing business to remain productive.

•**Enter religious holidays on your business calendar.** Avoid scheduling important meetings on holy days. If you have a conflict, do what you can to accommodate the individual's religious preferences without calling attention to why. Insensitive people disregard the religious holidays of other faiths by admitting, "I don't keep up with that stuff." There aren't that many holidays to consider, but they are important to those who choose to honor them.

•**Resist proselytizing and parading.** Although your religion may tell you to convert the masses, remain low key at work and lead by example. Constant public references to religious activities during work conversations are also inappropriate. Save this

Sensitivity to religious practices prevents uncomfortable, litigious, time-consuming problems.

talk for private discussion with people you know well.
- **Avoid belittling people's religion.** There can be snickers about what kind of religion people practice, the inconvenience it causes, the suggestion of "How weird," "How sad," or "Well, what do you expect?" Religious practices are protected by law, so you cannot require, for example, men to shave their beard or women to wear makeup when their religion prohibits it.
- **Reconsider invocations at business or civic club meetings.** Do we really need them? To have another's practice imposed on you in the workplace is offensive. If you choose to pray, and it is an option not to in these meetings, use prayers from other faiths or observe a moment of silence for an individual prayer offering. Resist the over-emphasis on Christianity.
- **Remember, not everyone celebrates Christian holidays.** Some Christians don't even celebrate popular Christian holidays; others have their own interpretations of celebration. Keep your best wishes for the holidays in the "Happy Holidays" category, rather than wishing business associates you don't know well, "Merry Christmas," or "Happy Easter."

Sensitivity to religious practices prevents uncomfortable, litigious, time-consuming problems. ■

Ann C. Humphries

Holy Days

Even with a regular business calendar and a multifaith wall calendar, I remain unsure about which religious holidays to honor when scheduling business. Because some religious holidays change from year to year, call churches and religion departments at colleges and universities to establish specific dates. To help you plan business or public events, the following information might be helpful.

• **Don't schedule meetings on holy days.** People may only attend services of their faith, or they may be active participants in the service. Also, realize that people may ignore their holidays, but it's their choice, not yours. Gale Field, a meeting planner with the Florida Engineering Society in Tallahassee says, "We consider our members and those holidays that would impose on their religious life. I try to become acquainted with holidays that would be a factor."

• **Mark your business calendar with prominent religious holidays.** Many calendars don't indicate them. Call local churches and temples, or a college's religious studies department for specific days or order a multifaith calendar. Contact "Multifaith Resources," 33 Arrowwood Place, Port Moody, British Columbia, Canada V3H4JI and telephone/fax 604-469-

Realize that people may ignore their holidays, but it's their choice, not yours.

1164.
Here are holidays to be aware of:
- Christianity—Christmas (always December 25) and usually Christmas Eve, Western Easter Sunday, Good Friday even Ash Wednesday, Maundy Thursday, and Palm Sunday. The Greek Orthodox Easter Holy Week falls at a different time than Western Easter. Not all Christians celebrate holidays. Jehovah's Witnesses only honor the Lord's Evening Meal which occurs around March.
- Judaism — Mark Rosh Ha Sha Nah, Yom Kippur, Passover, and the first night of Hanukkah. Jewish holidays run sunset to sunrise, so keep open the evening before.
- Islam — Mark Eid-ul-Fitr and the two days following, Eid-ul-Adha, and the First of Ramadan.
- Baha'i Faith — Naw Ruz which concludes The Nineteen Day Fast.
- Hinduism — Holi, Vaisakhi, and the most important, Diwali, Festival of Lights.
- Buddhism — New Year and Wesak, the Coming of Full Moon. ■

Ann C. Humphries

Dealing With the Issue of Age

Like gender or race, calling attention to people's age is unnecessary and, often, inappropriate. If you are tempted to disregard someone's contribution because they are young, remind yourself of the brilliant young pitchers for the Atlanta Braves. Just because people are young does not mean they cannot perform. Ever remarked at the youthful appearance of a police officer or physician, "You aren't even old enough to shave," or "You could be my daughter/granddaughter."

Also unnecessary are references to how old someone is, "She's well-preserved for her age," or "I must be getting old. I can't remember a thing. Yuk! Yuk!" In most social business contexts, age is irrelevant to consider or mention.

Also be careful not to misuse "Ma'am" and "Sir" in business contexts. Unless you are involved in personal, private business, such as delivering healthcare, taking a reservation, parking a car, or delivering a package, which requires some degree of detached, respectful formality, refrain from using "Ma'am" or "Sir" in the workplace. Even if you were brought up to address your elders respectfully, "Ma'am" and "Sir" raise an unnecessary reference to age. It also signals a rigid, provincial approach to business which is rarely flattering. While many people may disagree, I consider "Ma'am" and "Sir" to be only appropriate,

Once people reach the age of adulthood, they should address adults as adults to sound more professional and businesslike.

although not required, for children under age 18. Once people reach early adulthood, they should begin to break the habit of addressing adults with these honorifics. These words put too much distance between fellow business professionals. Abuses include some clerk on the phone or at a counter who barks, "Ma'am. MA'AM," to interrupt or correct you.

To show respect, use "Yessss" and "No" rather than "Yeah" or "Nu-uh," or simply use people's names. Regardless of their age, treat everyone with respect. ∎

Ann C. Humphries

The Sensitivities of Race

When the late Arthur Ashe was asked what his toughest adversary was, he didn't answer, "AIDS." He said, "Being black was. No question about it. Even now, it continues to feel like an extra weight tied around me."

Racism, both the obvious and the insidious, continues to be a problem. So many people deny their racist behaviors, yet progress can't be made until racist tendencies are acknowledged. The following guidelines can help when dealing with this sensitive issue.

• **Acknowledge that race is a factor.** Make it an open, credible topic of discussion. Rather than avoid the subject, undervalue it, or deny it, ask what can be done to address race issues. Monitor progress continuously.

"It's always an issue," says a black manager in manufacturing. "I know I'm more susceptible to being stopped for speeding, to being watched in a store, or to raising eyebrows when I arrive for meetings." Another professional relates, "We have to work at not being excluded from even small things such as going to lunch, being invited to receptions, or being appointed to projects."

Acknowledge that race is a factor. Make it an open, credible topic of discussion.

A white health care administrator says, "Never in my twenty years of professional life have I been more sensitive to race. I see direct evidence of how racial perceptions motivate, empower, and give hope for our staff—55 percent of whom are black. I need their contributions."

•**Be deliberate about representation.** Cynthia Legette, a PR consultant, says, "I appreciate when an effort is made for committees and boards to be racially diverse." Her approach is more diplomatic than, "Hey, you need more blacks in here," but don't be afraid to point out lack of diversity. The appointment of one minority does not rectify race issues. It can even highlight racial chasms.

Blacks usually feel they have their credentials challenged more than whites do, and that they must state their concerns more often and more convincingly to be heard. They resent hearing, "We could not find any qualified black candidates," over and over when they know of blacks with impeccable credentials. They resent being referred to in whispered tones as "the black" anything, or hearing whites proclaim, "I'm not racist," or "Some of my best friends are black."

We have a lot of work yet to do. Let's get to it. ∎

Ann C. Humphries

Let's Be Peacemakers

Lately, I've been wishing for a peacemaker, a person, or group that can create solutions, include not divide, unite not polarize, and honor differences not ridicule them.

Life today seems to force divisions. An air of mean-spiritedness prevails. Bullies are feared, but cheered. You are required to be for or against issues. Untruths are excused. Distrust exists, and that is saddening, disheartening and wearying.

On the other hand, when you think of it, we are facing bold new challenges. We are changing the course of history. Much of what we are doing and facing is revolutionary, a revolution fought with words, funding, and attention. This promise of change is exciting and invigorating, and the process cannot always be polite. Sometimes you have to shout or shock to get people's attention or make progress.

However, I wish to see myself develop more characteristics of a unifier, who does not repress, dilute, or trivialize, but who discusses what we can do, not what we can't do, where we agree, not where we disagree, and who respects and honors the opinions of others.

Think about your business life. How do you label people and ideas? Do you hear what people are telling you, or do you dis-

Do you hear what people are telling you, or do you dismiss them because of who says it or the way it is expressed?

miss them because of who says it or the way it is expressed? Where is agreement? What progress can you make? Anyone can call attention to problems. Let's raise the status of resolution. Let's be peacemakers.∎

The Right Moves, Volume II

Going Global

Ann C. Humphries

Canadian Business Customs

Attention to differences pays high dividends. As American communities attract business from Canada, more Canadians become their neighbors. As we receive these new neighbors into our communities, we should remember to pay attention to differences. To work well with Canadians as neighbors, customers, or employers, follow these guidelines.

•**Canadians are usually more formal than Americans.** They prefer a more measured tone of voice and a more precise demeanor. Say, "Thank you" instead of "Thanks," "Goodbye," instead of "Bye." Respond appropriately with a "You're welcome." Lori Bak, editor of *Meetings and Incentives Travel* in Toronto says, "A pet peeve of mine is that Americans often say 'U-huh' in response to my thanks. It seems as if they expect it."

•**Canadians value results or what you have done.** Promotional material should reflect what you can do rather than brag that you're the "greatest" or "the best" or that your service is "wonderful" or "fantastic." Be specific. Document.

•**Canadians are more reserved and circumspect than Americans.** They are private, respectful of form and feelings, and, thus, may seem aloof and suspicious. Criticism is diplomatic. Rather than complain, they may just walk away from the situation. Don't misinterpret this soft-spoken manner to be a

Attention to differences pays dividends, especially when dealing with people from other countries.

weakness nor expect loud praise from Canadians. Appreciation may be conveyed in more financial than verbal terms.

• **Canadians are Canadians, not American extensions.** Canadians have a rich heritage and are rightfully proud of it. Mark Simmons with the Chamber of Commerce in Columbia, South Carolina says, "Americans may be the biggest kid on the block, but not the only kids. Canadians are worthy of our respect. They see themselves as important partners in the North American market, not less than the United States." When you interact with Canadians, ask about their country; don't just talk about the United States. Learn some geography. Bak says, "American business people will refer to Toronto, Canada which is like my saying Miami, United States. Get the geography right."

• **Canadians are impressed by American friendliness.** "Especially in the South, people smile, notice when you enter their business, and seem to be genuinely interested in being helpful. We love it," says Bill Allison with Confederation Life Insurance Company in Atlanta, who spent years in Canada.

The subtleties of conducting business will make you more successful. Dismissing the differences is bad for business. ∎

Ann C. Humphries

Doing Business German Style

States and communities work diligently to attract new business to their area. Much of the effort targets international companies, and when these businesses begin operating, American workers may be confused or intrigued by different styles of work. Rather than expect international business people to become "Americanized" because they operate on our soil, smarter Americans pay attention to and honor the differences internationals bring.

For example, with high-profile companies such as BMW investing in South Carolina and Mercedes Benz locating in Alabama, Americans have a high stake in knowing how to work well with Germans. While Germans have long been conducting business in America, these highly visible announcements capture our attention.

Here are general guidelines that may help you understand German styles of conducting business.

• **Germans are deliberate.** Business meetings with Germans are to the point. They are planned and announced well in advance. They start at the precise time advertised and follow a strict, well-orchestrated agenda. Handshakes are firm, introductions formal, voices and facial expressions modulated, and posture erect. Germans use titles and rarely use first names even with friends. Their follow-through is extraordinary. Decisions

Smart Americans pay attention to and honor the differences internationals bring. They adjust to work with people from other countries.

are more centralized.

Advice to Americans: Don't call "spur of the moment" meetings, drop by, add an unplanned agenda item, brainstorm, joke, or chat. Say German names respectfully and don't feel suspicious about Germans who prefer surnames and titles even when you think they should allow you to call them "Hans" after awhile. Dress crisply. Don't bob, slouch, or sway in your seat nor remove your suit coat.

• **Germans are frank.** Germans will reply with a direct "Yes" or "No" and Americans, especially Southerners, usually like their "No's" a little softer. Americans can be shocked by Germans who will tell you exactly what they think. Because they have high expectations and are extremely well-organized and goal driven, German criticism is swift and specific.

And, Germans are usually embarrassed by compliments, so offering praise may be awkward, infrequent or even suspect. As a typical American worker who will work hard for praise and a little appreciation, you may be in for disappointment.

• **Germans value accomplishment, skills, and the process as much as the results.** Germans distrust things that don't take the appropriate amount of time. They disdain rhetoric when it does not have action or proof. They are not impressed with whom you know if you do not have credentials.

Be willing to adjust your American ways to work well with people from around the world. You won't lose your identity. You will receive more respect by being flexible. ■

Ann C. Humphries

Style Matters In Latin America

Interest in conducting business in Latin America has boomed. But before you race to make your profits, heed this advice: Style matters.

"Style and manner are essential. The more gracious you are, the more receptive they are. Your sensitivity indicates you are thinking of their interests and benefits," says Roger Turner, United States Department of Commerce, Latin American Division, in Washington, D.C.

As large and diverse as Latin America is, it does have commonalties in business customs. Here are highlights.

1. Latin American business people are sophisticated. Americans often have the perception that a small economy, population, and geography mean a small mindset. Latin Americans are smart, well-educated, admirable business partners. Don't adopt patronizing tones or refer too often to how things are done in the United States. William F. Vartorella, an international consultant in Camden, South Carolina, says, "Latin Americans are formally informal." A breezy approach, superficial style, and shallow business plan won't work.

2. Relationships and reputation predominate. There is a saying, "In America, you do business with business. In Latin

"In America, you do business with business. In Latin America, you do business with people."

America, you do business with people." Latin Americans value reputation and trustworthiness. Face-to-face meetings and frequent contact with decision makers are vital. They resist rushing a relationship to cut a deal. Midstream shifts in personnel are mistrusted, and criticism is perceived as a personal insult. As part of respectful reciprocity, they expect pricing integrity and good service.

3. Time is important. It's spent differently. Time in Latin America is spent developing relationships. Quality of life and interests outside business are strong. Avoid showing impatience about someone arriving thirty minutes late without an apology. Resist tempting statements such as, "What? Another holiday?" or "This would never take this long in the U.S."

4. Communication styles are different. Latin Americans discount American directness as blunt and shallow. In contrast, Latin American communication is more indirect, elaborate, and complimentary. Because relationships are important, they may tell you what you want to hear, rather than risking offending you with the truth.

Becoming aware of how people in the U.S. compare and differ with Latin American styles of business will benefit you not just abroad but also here in the United States. ■

Ann C. Humphries

The Mexican Style Of Business

NAFTA's enactment has raised the curiosity of many American businesses about opportunities in Mexico. A common border and 86 million people continues to whet Americans' curiosity for business "south of the border." But, building business internationally isn't something you can risk with trial and error. The costs are too high.

To develop your business in Mexico more quickly, follow these techniques.

•**Pay attention to and honor the differences.** "There are cultural differences," says Kathy Marks-Gibler, a bicultural consultant in Monterrey, N.L., Mexico. "I've seen U.S. businesses never really see this as fact. Americans disregard the differences and choose to fly by the seat of their pants. That hurts their ability to do well here." For example, compared to Americans, Mexicans define themselves more broadly than their jobs or income. Family, religion, and quality of life are important.

•**Mexicans respond to authority differently.** In Mexico, status is important. Some Mexicans automatically respect their superiors and want authority figures to

Mexicans automatically respect their superiors and want authority figures to conduct themselves with dignity.

conduct themselves with dignity. Mexicans are offended by Americans who try to earn their respect through "shirt-sleeve" management, who talk with workers as equals, or disclose personal or professional limitations.

In addition, authority is centralized. Says Marks-Gibler, "Mexicans want to take up their individual concerns with the boss, and the boss will take the time to resolve the issue."

• **Teamwork is often difficult.** Because of their respect for authority and because Mexicans do not believe all people are created equal, they resist making independent judgments about their work. Instead, they prefer direction. U.S. companies wanting to pitch teamwork should realize cultural differences. Be patient with change.

One last word. Mexico is a large country. Just as there are differences in doing business in the Northeast, Midwest, West, and South here in the States, so are there differences in business in Mexico City, Guadalajara, and Monterrey. If you are sensitive to differences and adjust to the geographic and business climate, you will be much more effective and successful. ∎

Ann C. Humphries

Business, The Southern Way

Just as there are customs and styles of doing business with Canada, Mexico, and Japan, so are there business customs within the United States. Attune yourself to these customs, and you have a stronger chance to succeed.

The American South fascinates people. Mandy Romich, a graduate student from outside Washington, D.C. said, "Coming to the South is almost like going to London. Although we speak the same language, you definitely feel the culture shock."

Since more people are moving in and out of the South, here are a few observations to help people work better together and conduct business in the South.

• **Respect, don't ridicule.** Wherever you live, some of the culture differences are refreshing, some annoying, and others hilarious. Learn to appreciate what is distinctive. Don't criticize more than you compliment. This is home to many people. Bite your tongue when tempted to say, "How we do it up North" or "out West." Rethink preconceived notions that slow talkers are slow thinkers, or that the South is always behind. It's not.

• **Southerners are friendly, polite, and private.** The South has a formal informality about it. Many people are polite and

Southerners like to know where you are from and who you know before learning what you do.

friendly, but also private and formal. This is especially puzzling to outsiders who, after a stimulating visit, do not have invitations reciprocated or who consider nosy what Southerners consider friendly. Romich continues, "I surely didn't mean to come across as rude, but apparently by the way they looked at me, I did."

• **Southerners tend to be indirect, and relationships count.** Romich laughs, "I asked for directions, and I got a history of their relationship." Others say, "Southerners talk around things. All I wanted was a 'Yes' or 'No.'" Saving face is important which explains why Southerners will suggest, rather than direct. Conversations become, "You might want to consider..." "It's been suggested..." Sharp directness is perceived as rude; and fast talking, mistrusted. Unpleasantness and criticism are often difficult, and Southerners like to know where you are from and who you know before learning what you do.

Recognizing and honoring different customs and styles of doing business even within our own country sharpen the tools you can use to develop your business. ∎

Ann C. Humphries

Broad Generalizations

The historical handshake between PLO Chairman Yasser Arafat and Israeli Prime Minister Yitzak Rabin cast a soft beam of light into the rigid, dark chasm of fixed perceptions and impossibility. Suddenly people are seen differently. Anything is possible. There is hope.

We, too, must see people in our workplace, in our neighborhoods, and on our committees in different lights.

In honor of this historic agreement, for a moment at least, suspend your broad generalizations. Like the Palestinians and the Israelis, re-evaluate how you perceive people. Reconsider the phrases you use that discredit others, phrases heard in private asides or homogenous conversations that begin with, "You know those.... "Baptists," "...Catholics," "...Southerners," "Yankees," the "college graduates," "blue collar workers," "lower class," those "Republicans," "Democrats," "liberals," "conservatives," "lawyers," "pro-choice radicals," "pro-lifers," or attitudes like "They're too young," "They've been here too long," "A black could never work that territory," "A woman could never handle those people," "Men are all alike," and on and on.

Haven't you been in conversation with people who

When the world is changing and changing and changing, give yourself and the people around you more room to succeed.

disparage the very group of which you or people close to you are a member? Have you let slide cutting remarks that should have been addressed and redirected?

When the world is changing and changing and changing, give yourself and the people around you more room to succeed. Success is often in the lifting up, not the tearing down. ■

The Right Moves, Volume II

Dealing With Difficult People

Handling Nosy People

People can be so nosy. Their boldness can shock you as much as their lack of contrition for asking questions better left unasked. When you choose not to reply, they mutter, "Boy, is he touchy; it was an honest question," or "What is she hiding?"

We often witness news interviews where public figures are barraged by intrusive questions, then harassed for not answering. Some people view nosiness as a means to an end. Moreover, what is personal in one culture may be viewed as friendly in another.

Sooner or later, everyone must deal with the unbridled curiosity of a nosy person. The key is not to fall victim to the same temptations. As outgoing as Americans are, even we have our limits as to what is personal and what isn't.

Here are some guidelines for avoiding and handling nosy questions.

• Nosy questions usually surround issues regarding age, money, religion, politics, health, sex, reproduction, romance, and appearance. Expect to upset people when you ask questions like "How old is she?" "Why did you leave?" "How much did you pay?" "How did you vote?" "What rate did you get?" "How much was the settlement?" "Is that your real baby?"

When asked a nosy question, feign innocence and say "I beg your pardon?" or exclaim "I BEG your pardon!"

"What did you do over the weekend?" "Is it terminal?" "Are those real?" and "Putting on a few pounds?"

- Pay attention to the questions you ask and the reaction you get. Some people may intentionally not answer your question. When you ask the second time and they fog their answer, take a hint. Preview potentially personal questions and respect that people may not choose to reply. If people react to your questions with silence, stares, or shock, retreat rapidly and apologize.

- When someone asks you a question you consider intrusive, feign innocence and say "I beg your pardon?" or exclaim a commanding "I BEG your pardon!" or brush off the question with a "That's quite personal," or "Surely you did not mean to ask that," and change the subject. You can also give a general answer such as "A fair price," but to be most effective, use words. Withering stares and cold silences are vague. Be specific, frank, and verbal, not mean-spirited, or the crowd will turn against you.

At times, the natural curiosity of people overrules their good manners. Don't let it happen to you. Develop tactful responses to uncomfortable or inappropriate questions. ■

Ann C. Humphries

Disagreeing With People

Many business people remain confused, even timid, about how to disagree with people or how to correct inappropriate behavior. Much too often, we leave issues unchallenged. When we refuse to throw down the gauntlet, patterns can develop and problems grow.

Consider, for instance, the abusive senior manager. She was brilliant, but the staff and her peers were demoralized working with her. She had been warned to stop the shouting, but she remained in her job, making no changes in her behavior and avoiding the consequences.

Other examples include a usually articulate woman who said nothing when the guests at a dinner party ridiculed an individual she respected, and an accomplished attorney who chose to leave a job rather than confront unethical conduct and crass, sexual remarks.

Heard of co-dependent behavior? This is it. When you allow people to do things you do not want, you are part of the problem. By not saying anything, you allow behaviors to continue.

Here is what you can do.

• **Address the problem.** We all respect a person who is astute and confident enough to address issues we might not even see.

Your reputation is more than what you stand for. It is also what you won't stand for.

When a behavior occurs more than once, honor your instincts and raise the issue. If you ignore it, it will continue.

- **Ask for clarification.** When someone says something that is vague, but definitely smacks as unprofessional or inappropriate, ask for more detail. "When you said that, Keith, what did you really mean? What are you trying to say?" You alert them that you heard the underlying message they are projecting.
- **Be specific and look them in the eye.** Tell people, "This is what we mean by appropriate dress" and show pictures. Recite specific words, incidences, and dates of the offending behavior. Express how you feel, "When you said this today in the meeting, this is how it came across..." "When you do this, this is how I feel," then, tell people what you want them to do... "I want you to stop. If you don't stop, then this is what we will do," and mean it.

We continue to hear the ringing of, "If you can't say anything nice, don't say anything at all," "Give them enough rope, and they will hang themselves," or "Ignore it, and it will go away."

Much too often, we leave things unchallenged. Your reputation is more than what you stand for. It is also what you won't stand for. ∎

Ann C. Humphries

Addressing Rude People

You do have options for dealing with rude people. If you've ever said, "I didn't say anything, because I didn't want to appear rude," or "I just didn't know what to do," or if you've slammed down the phone, stomped around the office, or cursed in traffic because of how someone treated you, then read on. Here are tips for dealing with rude people.

• **Interrupt.** When speakers grandstand, move very, very close to them, then interrupt, "Chris, this has been great. Unfortunately we are out of time, but you'll be available during the break if anyone would like to talk with you, right? Now, our next order of business..." Interject in committee meetings to say, "Great point. We need to move on." Stop mean-spirited conversations to say, "You know, I don't find them to be that way at all."

• **Ask for clarification.** When someone gives you what borders on a smart reply, you might ignore it the first time, but when it occurs again, ask, "I beg your pardon?" or "I'm sorry. I didn't understand. Would you explain what you meant?" Silence, pauses, and slow stares can express a lot.

• **Initiate frank talks.** If someone speaks to you in a demeaning tone, let them know. "I'm trying to solve a problem here.

Being polite does not mean being weak. You can address rudeness, be firm, clear and definite, and maintain your dignity and power.

When you roll your eyes, call me 'Lady,' and keep me waiting for over an hour, I have a problem with that. This is what I want....." In the office, begin with, "Did you really mean what you said in that meeting?" or "Look. We need to talk. When you do this, we are affected in this way. I recommend these changes be made." Be specific and follow up.

- **Band together.** When an individual continues to act rudely, ask around to see if others are having similar problems. Get in a group and express your concerns together, "Here we are. This is what is happening. These are the problems that result, and this is what we recommend," and "Would you like to take this to the next level, or can we just settle this simply?"
- **Name names.** When people treat you inappropriately and you have followed reasonable protocol, go public. Write letters, file grievances, call the paper, or authorities. Out in the sunlight — revealed to a broader audience — inappropriate behavior has difficulty surviving.
- **Ask people to leave.** We've all been in situations when we have had to say, "I think you had better leave," or "Stop this car. I want out." Reassign people who cause problems in particular areas. Have the courage to fire.

Being polite does not mean being weak. You can address rudeness, be firm, clear and definite, and maintain your dignity and power. ∎

Handling A Bully

Bullies don't just appear in the school yard; they also emerge in the office. They can be your coworkers, sales people, even your boss. Unchecked or unmanaged, bullying behavior can increase. The consequences of bullying behaviors are an unmotivated staff, lost productivity, high turnover, and potential lawsuits. A recent southeastern Court of Appeals judgment awarded $28,000 to a boy and his mother because a teacher failed to manage the behaviors of two bullies in the classroom. Courts also hold companies responsible for suppressing bullying or harassing behaviors at work.

If a bully holds sway in your office, here is what you can do.

•**Identify bullying behavior.** Decide that certain behaviors are bullying. To label and define these behaviors makes your job easier. Don't doubt yourself.

•**Let bullies know how you feel.** Use language they will understand. Bullies can taunt and be openly mean, or they can cry, pout, or shun you. Bullies do not respond to kind suggestions in squeaky voices nor do they get the hint through joking. You can approach this lightly with, "Could I talk with you a minute? You know, when you do this, this is how it comes

Employees who say, "I'm not the type of person to confront a bully" invite bullying and become part of the problem.

across, and you might try another approach before it misrepresents who you are." Be direct, "I see what you are doing. I find it unprofessional. It doesn't work with me. I want it to stop."

•**Develop your plan of action.** You have many options to stop the behavior. If there is no response or you receive ridicule, add your next step. Involve others. Go in a group to say, "We're all onto you. You can stop now." Take it up the ladder until you get some resolution. Employees who say, "I'm not the type of person to confront" invite bullying and become part of the problem. Employers who laugh off the behavior, tell employees to work it out, develop a tougher skin, or say the people really didn't mean it personally are also part of the problem.

Bullying is a common behavior in many work settings. That doesn't mean you have to ignore or endure it. Practice strategies that enable you to manage bullies. ■

Dealing with Snipers

Here's a situation more common than you'd think. The corporate office staff makes snide remarks concerning a manager who's discussing a quality program being tested. Instead of supporting the program, the corporate staff rolls their eyes and issues comments such as, "Well, he operates in a closed environment and can dictate what happens," or "She has high expectations. We all know about her opinions."

There are two issues in this situation. The first is the arrogance and self-importance that can arise in quality programs. Abusers of quality programs tell you how to work with them, label people as uncooperative when they disagree, and resent your raising issue with how the quality office conducts itself. If you are managing a quality program, place checks on yourself to avoid abuse.

The second issue is one regarding snipers. Snipers attack unexpectedly from protected vantage points. They talk about people who are absent. They seek to undermine a person's credibility, and they are skilled at sliding in veiled remarks or embarrassing people in front of others.

When this happens to you or someone else, recognize it. Ask for clarification. "What do you mean by that?" "Did I hear you

You must address snipers, otherwise you appear to condone their behavior.

say...." "Why do you say that?" The cowards will probably backpedal, "Oh no, no, no, that's not what I meant. What I meant was...." but you will have put them on notice that you understood, and you want clarity and proof. You will listen to substantiated comments and specifics, but not to innuendo.

Another strategy is to seek confirmation. Ask others you trust for their reaction. "Mary, this was said. I'm uncomfortable with it. What do you think?" Trust your perceptions of inappropriate behavior. Tell people in charge, "This is what was said in the meeting, and I'm uncomfortable with it. I want to know your reaction." You must address the snipers, otherwise you appear to condone the behavior. ∎

Standing Your Ground

Stop feeling guilty when you address someone else's inappropriate behavior. Resist replaying how you made your point especially to someone who tends to be insensitive. Reflect and apologize, perhaps, for a crude delivery, but don't let them wriggle out of the issue.

Betsy has an important job as a university administrator, but when determining how and when to confront a colleague who eats up her time shooting the breeze, she gives inordinate thought to, "Well, I don't want to be rude."

Hector finally tells a pestering co-worker who presses for an opinion to, "Shove it," whereupon the co-worker mocks Hector in the break room. Chris politely overlooks the inappropriate behavior of a friend, then hints around it until one shift when he finally explodes, "I want you to stop this." His friend sobs, "You are so mean and hurtful," and Chris is tempted to coddle the friend.

The examples go on and on. Many accomplished, respected professionals hesitate to act out of concern for hurting or embarrassing the very people who have been rude and disrespectful to them. Stop doubting or undermining yourself.

Even with thorough introspection, months of deliberation

Stop punishing yourself with guilt. Instead, believe in your and others' ability to find a better way.

and pause, painstakingly working within the system, and a tactful, calculated delivery, confrontation can still get ugly. Issues are not easy. There is no prescription. On many issues, people simply will not want to hear what you have to say. They will argue rather than seek to understand. They deny allegations and rationalize their behavior (yours, too).

The process is scary. Your heart can grow mighty heavy, but take strength. While some people get great results with inbred diplomacy or unapologetic boldness, others learn expensive lessons by trial and error. They realize, at some point, the only way to resolve an issue is to work through it, however, rough, unpleasant or risky.

Whether addressing the inappropriate behavior of an individual or a group, stop punishing yourself with guilt. Instead, believe in your and others' ability to find a better way. ■

Dealing With Upset People

If you feel you deal with the rudest, meanest people around, consider how you might be contributing to the problem. If people feel *you* are insensitive to them, their anger could be justified. Here are some actions you can take to avoid having the problem escalate.

• **Acknowledge people.** When people approach your desk or service area, don't ignore them; greet them. Nod to the third or fourth person in line. They will appreciate your noticing them and will be exceedingly more patient with you. Return phone calls and respond to personal correspondence. People become incensed if they feel you are ignoring them.

• **Accommodate people.** Rather than forcing everyone to follow your policies and procedures, especially customers, consider treating people with special needs differently. A situation that may not be an emergency to you can be to another person. When people seem restless, find out why and help them. They may have a deadline, a plane to catch, or some other appointment.

• **Show sensitivity.** People can become livid if you state your policy in a robot-like voice or clinch your teeth and say, "Well, SIRRR, we require you to fill out...." or "You must..." or "We

Tell people what you can do for them, not what you can't. Ask what you can do to satisfy upset people.

must have..."

Instead, acknowledge their plight with, "I can see this has upset you," or "This must be a terrible inconvenience." Avoid saying what you *can't* do. Focus instead on what you can do. "We can store your luggage, and you can use the pool or visit the shopping mall next door until our 4 p.m. check-in time."

• **Honor commitments.** Americans are extremely sensitive about commitments and follow through. People expect you to honor a price you quoted, come when you say you will, and make a delivery when promised. If you can't honor commitments, alert people to avoid surprises. Apologize for delays and consider a small restitution.

• **Seek solutions.** Ask what you can do to satisfy upset people. Too often, we fear people may ask the unreasonable. Their requests can be quite small. "I just want an apology," or "Please repair my machine. That's all I ask." If they ask for something you can't do, offer them a choice of what you can do. "We can't give you a free room, but we can buy you lunch or two buckets of range balls."

When you handle upset people with tact, sensitivity and aplomb, they will view your intentions as sincere and can become loyal allies. Be attentive to upset people. Observers will take note when you handle delicate situations with dignity. ■

Excuses and Accountability

Results! We work to get results. While intentions are fine, the outcome is what counts.

Think about when a person hurt you or your business, but professed, "I didn't mean any harm."

If the damage is great enough, they must be accountable for the results, not their intent. If an accident results in extreme loss, the person or company causing the accident becomes accountable. If a person with a gun admits, "I didn't mean to kill..." they still are accountable for the outcome. If a person is sloppy, neglectful, or uninformed with their practices, they, too, must be accountable, even if they did not mean to cause a problem. Of course, good intentions and acts of nature are considered, but so is negligence in determining restitution or punishment.

In business, be more vigilant about being accountable. Enthusiasm does not always work. People who promise a lot and raise expectations need to be aware of what they can deliver. People who preface hurtful or offensive remarks with, "I don't mean to offend anyone, but...." cannot excuse the results of what they say and how they say it. Institutions which practice policies that, although unintentionally, penalize certain

If a person is sloppy, neglectful, or uninformed with their practices, they, too, must be accountable.

groups need to re-evaluate their strategies.

"We didn't mean to," is not always an acceptable excuse. Become more accountable. ■

Apologies - Receiving and Giving

Senator Robert Packwood's apology for harassing female staffers and Marge Schott's for racist remarks made headlines. Corporate responses from WAL-Mart and Food Lion addressing accusations of inappropriate business practices intrigued us, too.

Apologies emerge regularly on the front page and at the watercooler. They are interesting for the effect they have on an individual or company's reputation, and they can provide insight into the future of a career, character of an individual, or the strength of a business.

People have clear expectations as to what makes an effective apology. Here's what seems most important.

• **When receiving an apology, people expect it to be sincere.** People define sincerity by saying they expect it to be a clear acknowledgement of what was done and an admission that it had a negative effect on people. They want this information without excuses.

What angers people is for someone to ignore their complaint, offer distractions, or trivialize their concern. When someone excuses their actions with, "I was under the influence of alcohol," or "That's the way people of my generation talked," or "Those are standard practices," you react as a seasoned hospital administrator responded, "That may be the reason, but that's still no excuse."

Handling apologies well is one of the most difficult things an individual or company must do. Done well, it is a mark of character.

People also become "ballistic" when others undervalue their concerns with statements such as, "Hey, it wasn't that big a deal. Why are you so upset?" People also hold others and businesses in low esteem when they accuse the accuser, whine about being unfairly targeted, or rail about all the good they have done.

• **What makes apologies effective is admitting what's wrong.** What makes them even more effective is that companies or individuals also offer restitution. We remember the full page ads American Airlines ran several years ago apologizing for the inconvenience of a strike. We admire the quick, determined response of Johnson and Johnson to pull all Tylenol from the shelves. Attempting to maintain a low profile or insulting people who ask you to address questionable practices can explode on you. The public can be very smart. Admitting problems (and how you'll correct them) can silence even the strongest critics.

Handling apologies well is one of the most difficult things an individual or company must do, but when done well is a mark of character. ■

The Right Moves, Volume II

Company Manners

Ann C. Humphries

Admirable Workplace Behaviors for Employees

Business could be conducted much more effectively if the people in charge clarified their expectations, and if the people who reported to them honored these expectations.

A recent survey asked: "What behaviors do bosses, team leaders, and supervisors appreciate in the people who report to them?" Here are the prominent responses.

• **Honesty** — Once again, readers listed honesty as a dominant characteristic of workplace behavior. Honesty can be expressed in completing time sheets, restating what happened truthfully, in not overselling yourself, and in offering ways to improve.

• **Self-starter** — People in charge appreciate people who take initiative to learn new skills or do new jobs, who are responsive and exercise judgment to solve problems, and who anticipate and handle what needs to be done. One reader expresses, "I appreciate when they relieve my load rather than heap more on me."

• **Team Player** — Respondents listed people who are flexible, who honor their co-workers' positions, who are easy to be

Flexible people who honor their co-workers' positions and seek not to grandstand contribute to the workplace.

around, who seek not to grandstand but to contribute, and who consider the benefits to a group as valued characteristics.

Other characteristics listed are punctuality, good attitude, pride in work, friendliness, respect, and optimism.

Behaviors bosses do not appreciate include:

- **Not honoring time** — Tardiness, procrastination, poor attendance, too much personal business at work, and gossiping steal time from work.
- **Lack of concern** — Not taking the initiative, laziness, refusal to help saying, "It's not my job," or an attitude of, "What's in it for me?" project a lack of concern. Also in this category are employees who make excuses or pass blame.
- **Poor professional appearance** — Loud cologne or excessive perfume, gum popping, talking loudly, untidy work area, shorts at work (even short sets), and inappropriate dress for the work environment convey an unprofessional image.

Also listed by managers as undesirable characteristics of employees were dishonesty, unfriendliness, negative attitude, unwillingness to accept change, and lack of dependability. ■

Ann C. Humphries

Employee Expectations Of Managers

Readers responded to a survey which asked what they value in their managers. Their responses follow.

• **Honesty** — Honesty is interpreted by not overselling what you can do, by being frank, and in keeping numbers accurate. Anyone who cheats on the golf course, on their time sheet, in withholding important information, inaccurately reporting it, or taking credit for something they didn't do is dishonest.

Related to this is the ability to honor confidences. One person said her boss opened her response to a confidential survey, then refused to turn it in. Another told of a boss repeating a confidential conversation in public. Honesty is important to employees.

• **Shows appreciation** — Employees are desperate for their contributions to be acknowledged. They work more earnestly when their work is appreciated. Writing a note or mentioning progress is an inexpensive motivator.

Several respondents mentioned that they like a boss who does not feel threatened when an employee is recognized. Two situations were mentioned where bosses didn't attend employee recognition celebrations because of jealousy.

• **Respects employees** — Employees want bosses to let them

Employees appreciate a supervisor who takes time to explain things and does not show favoritism.

do the jobs for which they were hired. They want support when they are right, not blind support which, as one respondent wrote, "may lead me over a cliff. I want to be protected from bad decisions, too." Employees want acknowledgement of personal issues which need attention and specifically mention demanding family situations. They appreciate a supervisor who takes time to explain things and who does not show favoritism.

• **Exceptional and respectful listening** — Respondents appreciated managers who listened to what employees were saying, considered new sides of an issue, and took time with people.

• **Self-importance** — They specifically listed managers who perceived themselves as being above the rules, self-centered, and unwilling to celebrate the achievements of their staff.

• **Abuses of staff** — Readers also cited supervisors who blame all for the errors of one, belittle and harass the staff, show favoritism, and use employees against each other. They note managers who neglect their work and their staff, who do not give employees the benefit of their judgment, or who do not back them when they act independently.

Respondents were very clear about what they expected and what they objected to in managers. Their list benefits everyone. ■

When Leadership Changes

Every four years, we have the opportunity to elect a new president. Similar opportunities for new leadership occur in business settings. A change in leadership can occur suddenly or can come after a lengthy campaign. Perhaps a significant public organization in your community has had turnover as a result of retirement, reorganization, or firing.

Regardless of its reasons or time frames, when a leadership change takes place, people see the change as a new day, and they have their own priorities. Here's what people say they'd like from new leaders.

• **"We'd like to be heard."** Readers wanted the opportunity to reintroduce themselves and their concerns. In older organizations where patterns had been established and groups labeled as favored or disfavored, the simple request for input helps people feel honored, and as a result, motivated.

People, however, do not want a series of questionnaires which further distance leaders from employees. As one worker put it, "So what if it's not scientific, we want someone who will listen and respond to us and what we are trying to say."

Some workers want decisions and forthrightness. They want new leadership to respect old ways.

- **"We want the dead wood out."** With a new approach and perspective, staff wanted to remove materials and people that inhibit productivity. What old organizations overlooked, new organizations can honor and act to change.
- **"We want decisions, action, and leadership."** Some workers said they wanted new leadership to be respectful of old ways, not slash the workplace. They appreciated being asked for input, but they also wanted decisions and forthrightness. "They don't have to be our friends. We know they won't do everything we suggest, but we do want to see a sign they can lead us where we need to go."
- **"We want feedback. We want to be included."** After their initial solicitation for input, employees want to know what the plans are. They want to contribute to healthy change. They did not like the pallor of silence or the selective inclusion of certain groups over others. "We want the new person in charge to be accessible, to give us direction, to ask for our input, and be with us. That's how we work best." ∎

Downsizing With Grace

As companies reorganize, merge, or downsize, many employees lose their jobs. For those who remain, it's not easy being one of the survivors. A common response from survivors, "I don't want to talk about it."

I have written many columns, but I've never been more puzzled, then moved, by people's reluctance to discuss being one of the few to remain after downsizing. Most wanted their remarks approved by their company before release. They referred me to the public relations department. Several simply said, "No comment."

Staying with a company after a reorganization and a downsizing is an extremely sensitive subject, and some didn't want to jeopardize their jobs. No one said, "I'm able to get more done," "I've found new ways to do things," or that "Work was a pleasure."

Instead, one responded, "I'm grateful to have a job. It's not the job I wanted, but, hey, it is a job." She continued, "I've come to value what is important, and things I used to worry about don't bother me anymore, not in contrast to the unemployment so many of my friends have experienced."

"Just wait until this recession if over," said another.

During times of recession and crunch, the challenge is to get more done.

Several readers commented about how "bone-tired we all are." They said the workload had increased without supporting resources. The stress of not knowing what to say or where to place loyalties has created an exhausted, demoralized staff.

One bright manager who considered resigning to start his own business said, "All my staff meetings are now encouragement sessions. That's all I can give them. I keep thinking, 'If I can just hold on,' but I don't know how much longer I can withstand this. We are all afraid. Just wait until this recession is over."

Staying with a company after a reorganization and a downsize is an extremely sensitive subject, and you do not want to jeopardize your job. During times of recession and crunch, if and when downsizing hits your company, remember, the challenge is to get more done. Find new ways to do things and search for ways to make work a pleasure. ∎

Ann C. Humphries

Families Who Work Together

Whether in the White House or a small family-owned business, special concerns arise when relatives work together. Families can work well together as husbands and wives, as in-laws, or as parents and children. The key to working well together is to avoid direct-line reporting and to resist overt favoritism or special privileges. Separate business from personal life and refrain from public displays of affection. Hold family to the same high company standards observed by other employees.

Family members should consider excusing themselves from certain meetings or assignments when their presence suppresses the free exchange of information. Families work best when their members' contributions are up to company standards and when inferior work is corrected. Relatives should be open about their relationships, neither disguising themselves as just another employee nor using their name as leverage for preferential treatment.

Family members who have impeccable credentials and work extra hard to quiet office talk, prove themselves as deserving of promotions and respect.

Families do not work well in business when they directly

Family members should be sensitive to others when their presence suppresses the free exchange of information.

report to each other, when their credentials are inferior, when the family overlooks substandard work or overreacts to criticism involving their relatives. Weak relatives can become pawns of other employees, and morale and employee trust can run dangerously low if employees feel the family member is a spy.

Relatives who work together should pay special attention to separating their personal lives from their business relationships. ∎

Ann C. Humphries

Mixing Friends and Business

Mixing friendship with business can prove to be risky. We've seen prominent political and business figures supported, then damaged by friends. You can probably remember a business situation thrown into chaos when the boss's friend entered the picture.

As newly elected political administrations review their teams, as giants in corporate America reorganize, and as we read about bruised ethics in government and business, we see vivid examples of the need for delineating friendship and business.

People surveyed about the issue of working with friends had important points to make.

• **Don't do it.** Three professionals called with blunt warnings for those considering going into business with or hiring friends. One stated, "You could lose your friendship and, worse, your business. I know. I made the mistake." Another said, "When you hire friends, your judgment is handicapped, criticism is tricky, and emotions run high."

"Friendships may develop from a business affiliation," adds a third, "and continue after the business association is over, but the respect for the business relationship should remain distinct."

• **Keep business relationships more formal than friendships.** A few readers described how the support of friendships

Keep business relationships more formal than friendships.

can evolve in the office and how fun it is doing things together after work. "If people can maintain some formality and resist playing favorites or creating cliques, no problem," writes one reader.

Still another says, "There is too much over-familiarity today. Why must we become so involved with each other at work? It borders on social harassment."

To negotiate the potential mines of friendships in business, guard against extending business discussions through the vehicle of personal conversation. Resist expecting favors and preferential treatment. Keep your work pace brisk and be willing to take criticism. ∎

Ann C. Humphries

Working With and Respecting Suppliers

How you work with, invest in, and—let's call it for what it is—respect suppliers can help you through hard times and important projects. This may come as a surprise to businesses who treat these professionals with suspicion and disdain, keep them at arms' length, and do not disclose what they want to accomplish.

Ineffective business people abuse suppliers, then complain they do not get good service. They view suppliers as adversaries, and therefore abuse appointments with sales people, argue about the insignificant, pit one supplier against another, and let price, not service or quality dominate. For a few dollars, they multiply, rather than reduce their work by interviewing and buying from many suppliers, which then requires someone's valuable time to review prices and services, handle invoices, and write checks.

Smart business people know the value of working together with suppliers. They build relationships. They use suppliers' counsel for product knowledge, market conditions, and industry innovations. They recognize and develop suppliers as insur-

Difficult clients pay for their attitude. They pay by missing extra service or quiet discounts.

ance for emergencies or special requests, for suppliers come to the aid of good clients.

Here's another surprise to those who buy. Difficult clients pay for their attitude. They pay by missing extra service or quiet discounts. Suppliers may not even be as available, for suppliers pick their customers, too.

To get the best in service, product, and pricing, invest in suppliers. Respect them. Honor their time. Reveal what you really want and ask for their help in solving problems. Listen to their suggestions for better ways to work together. Don't just tell them how to work better with you. Be willing to pay a fair price and to thank them occasionally for their support and good work. ■

Poor Morale — Learn From It

Bad employee attitudes may have worthy origins. When morale is bad, better look to the generals, not just the troops.

In times of depressed business conditions, everyone suffers; but when management uses pressure tactics on employees as a form of punishment, results rarely come. Instead, morale plummets. Initiative stops.

David McCullough's award winning book, *Truman,* profiled the evolution of the Korean War and how General MacArthur told President Truman and his staff that they must proceed beyond the 38th parallel to stop the Chinese. MacArthur was emphatic about driving north and attempted to use low troop morale as leverage. However, Secretary of State George Marshall advised that MacArthur examine his own leadership style, that troop morale is dependent upon the leader.

Truman continued, "MacArthur needs to stop seeing us as the enemy." The new general, Matthew Ridgeway, reported that troop morale was not an issue, that basic living conditions were. He made sure they had decent food and shelter, accessible MASH units, and more protection. He moved among the troops, listened to them, and transformed old systems that limited progress into efficient resources to do the job. Morale

Talk to employees and honor their concerns. They aren't necessarily the enemy; they can be resourceful allies.

soared, and later the war ended.

There is a lesson in this story for business. When attitudes are bad, there may be good reasons. What in your business or organization is its own enemy? Do faulty systems or policies slow productivity? Do sacred cows or favorites need to be examined?

Re-evaluate leadership styles. The art of leadership is in motivating the troops and getting results. When turnover is high and productivity low, the wrong person may be in charge or inappropriate techniques being used.

Rather than bully, talk to employees and honor their concerns. They aren't necessarily the enemy; they can be resourceful allies. They may tell you what you really need to know. Larry King says in one of his books, "If you are perceived as having a lot of clout, you have to let people around you know it's okay to be honest with you. I make allowances for my staff to tell me when I'm off base."

The lesson from etiquette is to treat people respectfully. Honor employees as human beings. Be approachable, listen to their concerns, and don't bully. ∎

The Benefits Of A Light Touch

Even in these days of candidness and forthrightness, agendas and results, a light touch is refreshing. Earl Hewlette, managing partner of Wild Dunes Resort near Charleston, South Carolina, has a light touch. "I'm sensitive to intimidating through the force of my personality coupled with an authoritative position of senior management. To get everybody's best effort and focus on a solution, I want them relaxed and contributing. If they are self-conscious about looking foolish or making a mistake, I lose the benefits of their knowledge, instincts, and intuition, and that's a mistake. I find I often mediate discussion, rather than lead it."

Softer voice tones, indirectness, laughter, and simply trusting the intelligence and intent of the group can be a more effective strategy than stating the obvious.

A heaviness can permeate when you find yourself continuously driven or purposeful.

Sometimes, a light touch gives people room to operate, air to breathe, and opportunities to contribute. Pacing enables concepts and relationships to develop and flower, and in business, relationships mean profitability, productivity, and results.

Business customs of other cultures give insight to this

Don't be deceived by a light touch. It can belay superior intelligence, insight, and strength.

strategy. People within groups of native Americans, Japanese, Canadians, even some Californians excel in understatement, intentionally leaving things unfinished or unplanned, inquiring about you to relax you, and relying upon what is not said to communicate a message. They understand the influence of heritage and the power of atmosphere and location to control events and motivate people.

A light touch is not rambling, sloppy, or shallow. Modifiers such as "perhaps," "you might want to consider," or indirectness isn't necessarily evasive or weak. Instead, they may be deliberate ways to guide you to a point. Indirectness can sometimes be a more sophisticated path to influencing and motivating than perseverance, thoroughness, or forcing an issue.

Don't be deceived by a light touch. It can belie superior intelligence, insight, and strength. ■

Ann C. Humphries

Graceful Transitions

Every four years, Inauguration Day enables us to witness examples of grace: refreshing, inspiring grace. Grace is a reflection of personal character supported by basic, unpretentious manners and politeness. Manners prepare us for situations that demand the best of us. Grace and manners also protect us from acting inappropriately or disrespectfully when the occasion or people might tempt or overwhelm us.

According to Dunbar Godbold, staff dentist with the Veteran's Administration, "Politeness seems so lacking today. I don't understand why people don't value it more. It allows us to treat each other with respect and worth. Once established, we can conduct our business and develop a relationship. Without it, we can't seem to progress."

Here are a few examples of grace, manners, and politeness noticed during President Clinton's Inauguration.

•**White House greeting.** Both the Bush and Clinton families were respectful and sensitive to each other during this most emotional moment.

•**Praise of Mr. Bush during the Inaugural Address.** President Clinton's recognition of his predecessor's "fifty year's of service" was genuine and sincere. It could easily have been

Grace is a reflection of personal character supported by basic, unpretentious manners and politeness.

patronizing or overdone.
- **Names correctly pronounced.** The official who presided over the ceremonies correctly pronounced Dr. Maya Angelou's name. (AN-JA-LO)
- **Goodbye's to the Bushes.** President and Mrs. Clinton walked the Bushes to the helicopter and waited while it ascended. Often, as their guests leave, people close their doors before their guests are gone.

People with good manners walk their guests to the front door of their office. In their homes, they escort them to the sidewalk or watch from the door as their guests drive away.
- **Not engaging in disparaging remarks.** Mrs. Bush would not engage in criticism of Mrs. Clinton. She just would not.
- **Waiting until the end.** The Inaugural Parade started and ended late, but the members of the Presidential Viewing Box stayed until the end, responding enthusiastically to even the last participants.

Both the Bushes and the Clintons conducted themselves with dignity and grace which should serve as an example for all of us. ∎

Retiring With Grace

Retiring from a job takes skill. With many people accepting incentives for early retirement in both the public and private sectors, a review of etiquette for the retiree and the organization may be helpful.

To the retiree:

• **Keep your retirement to yourself until you are ready to go public.** Resist the temptation to threaten to retire, "In a few months, I could be out of here," or "If I don't get the support or respect I deserve, I'm leaving." Your supervisor may know, but you can both decide to keep it quiet until closer to the actual departure date. Then, consider sending out announcements to let business associates know of your plans and new address.

• **Keep your retirement letter positive.** This isn't a problem if you have had a happy stay, but if you have had an uneasy tenure, remember, the letter is permanent and remains in your files. You can address briefly the issues that concerned you; however, end with a note of praise.

• **Continue to work.** After you have announced your retirement, don't waste people's time with excessive personal talk or superficial work. Invest in or be available to the people who will inherit your work and help the transition.

Take care with retirement. Endings are just as important as beginnings

- **Stop by the old workplace occasionally, but develop a new life.** Resist making policy or criticizing from the outside.

To the employer:

- **Treat the person about to retire with respect.** Do not allow actions that undervalue them or their contributions. They still hold a job for which they are paid. Other staff will carefully observe your treatment of the soon-to-be retired. Phasing out projects and phasing in new people are to be understood, but adopting or allowing a patronizing attitude toward them or isolating them is not only in poor taste but bad business policy.
- **Include retirees in periodic company functions. Don't be wooden about it.**

Take care with retirement. Endings are just as important as beginnings. ∎

Ann C. Humphries

The Art of Leaving

As political terms expire, as years draw to a close, as the football season ends, prominent people leave office. Some, like Dan Reeves, (former coach of the Denver Broncos), are fired. Others such as Lee Iacocca retire, and others like former President Bush leave office because of election losses or expired terms.

Whether people serve in the national arena or occupy local positions in business or politics, whether their leaving is common knowledge or a sudden occurrence, whether they are ending their careers or tendering a routine resignation, there is an art to leaving office. When asked how people should conduct themselves as they leave their posts, here are some readers' responses.

•**Give the new people every chance to succeed.** One reader said, "Office holders enhance the legacy of their accomplishments when they set up the office for their successors to do well." Another called to say, "One of the best pieces of advice I ever heard was when, as a young lieutenant, a retiring colonel told me, 'Don't raise my name to the successor. Give him your best effort.'"

•**Check your tongue.** As tempting as it is to criticize, resist. Avoid "pot shots" at the organization or the people succeeding you. "Several of our board members became grouchy, impa-

How you treat people leaving office reflects on you. Avoid treating people as lame ducks and resist being pushy or patronizing.

tient, and mean-spirited as their terms expired," one reader responded. Another caller mentioned, "It is hard to work with people who continually remind you of how happy they will be to be gone."

•**Keep up the productivity.** When some people resign, they simply stop working. Months prior to retirement, some retirees are useless, because they withdraw, make lengthy tours to say goodbye, or schedule many farewell events. As we watched Mr. Bush handle Somalia and Saddam Hussein, we saw an individual maintain the power of the presidency until the end.

•**Respect the office you have held.** Beware of taking clients, confidential files, even small equipment with you. Watch how often you return or how much time you take up visiting.

How you treat people leaving office reflects on you, too. Avoid treating people as lame ducks or victims and resist adopting a manner that is pushy or patronizing. Until a short time before they depart, include people about to leave office in invitations or assignments. Call them periodically after they are gone. ∎

Ann C. Humphries

Good Endings

The business world emphasizes good first impressions; yet, how you finish is just as important as how you begin. Think about how people end things — jobs, projects, telephone conversations, even the the work day.

Today, the way telephone conversations end range from dribbling off, "Yeah, bye," to the perky, "Have a nice day," to high-pitched baby tones, "Byee, byeeee." What ever happened to "Goodbye, " or even better, "Goodbye, Mr. Jones"?

Don't you like to know when people leave? It's a simple professional courtesy to tell someone you are leaving, to notify people when you transfer your phone to their desk, even to say goodbye at the end of the day. These simple courtesies are not meant to restrict your freedom, but rather enable people to help you at work.

Then there are the issues of employees leaving the company, reorganizations, and reassignments. Connie Ginsberg, executive director with Family Connections, called a representative with whom she had been dealing for years to have the receptionist sheepishly murmur, "She's...ah...no longer with us. Susie Jones is now handling your account. Let me transfer you." Clunk. Ginsberg says, "Then, I was faced with the decision to spend

If you can end things as well as you begin them, your reputation and that of your company will soar.

time re-educating this new representative on the complexities of the project, and frankly I did not want to, especially the way the transfer was handled. If the former representative was unable to notify clients," continues Ginsberg, "the company surely should have. I have since changed companies to one that respects relationships."

In contrast, Becky Bailey, the new staff member of Partners of the Americas at Columbia College in Columbia, South Carolina, sent a memo to the organization's mailing list announcing her position, as "trying to fill the capable shoes of the former office holder," and she listed the former employee. This brief memo announced her association with Partners, the departure of former staff, and complimented their work. This simple task speaks well of her and the organization she represents.

Finally, there is the element of finishing a project. I appreciated the closing ceremonies of the Olympics. I admired the professionalism of Johnny Carson, Ed McMahon, and Doc Severinson as they finished their last programs. They invested in their last appearances as if their work would continue. They were attentive to the end. ■

ABOUT THE AUTHOR

ANN CHADWELL HUMPHRIES has written "The Right Moves" for The State since 1988. The column circulates to over 320 newspapers nationwide. As an author and speaker, she helps organizations and individuals refine the ways they conduct business. She is featured on South Carolina Educational Radio with "Manners Minutes." She and her husband Kirk, live in Columbia, South Carolina with their two sons, Brad and Charlie. This is her third book.

ETICON
ETIQUETTE CONSULTANTS FOR BUSINESS

ORDER FORM

	ITEM DESCRIPTION	UNIT PRICE	QUANTITY	TOTAL
BOOKS	**THE RIGHT MOVES, VOLUME II,** POPULAR EASY TO READ COLLECTION OF BUSINESS ETIQUETTE COLUMNS. SUGGESTIONS ON HOW TO HANDLE ALL OF THOSE DIFFICULT AND SOMETIMES AWKWARD SITUATIONS. EXCELLENT SOURCE OF REFERENCE.	$13.95		
	THE RIGHT MOVES, VOLUME I BUSINESS ETIQUETTE COLUMNS. A MUST FOR ANY BUSINESS PROFESSIONAL.	$10.00	SOLD OUT AVAILABLE SOON	
	ENOUGH OF THAT PHONY BUSINESS ENTERTAINING HANDBOOK OF UPDATED TELEPHONE STRATEGIES TO STRENGTHEN BUSINESS.	$15.95		
VIDEO	**PROUD TO BE POLITE,** A VIDEO BY KIDS, FOR KIDS AGE K-3RD GRADE. TEN SHORT MANNERS SEGMENTS. REAL, CHARMING. ADULTS AND CHILDREN ENJOY WATCHING. MAKES TEACHING MANNERS EASY AND ENTERTAINING.	$69.95 WITH GUIDE $49.95 VIDEO ALONE		
VIDEO	**"THE DOOR OPENS BOTH WAYS"** 26 MINUTES ON ETIQUETTE BETWEEN MEN AND WOMEN IN THE WORKPLACE. WITH HANDBOOK HANDBOOK ALONE RENTAL:	$79.95 $5.00 $40.00		
	SUBTOTAL: ADD PRICES OF ALL ITEMS ABOVE			
	SALES TAX: 5% SOUTH CAROLINA RESIDENTS ONLY			
	SHIPPING AND HANDLING			$5.00
	TOTAL: MAKE CHECKS PAYABLE TO **ETICON, INC.**			

MAIL TO P.O. BOX 69530, COLUMBIA, SC 29223-8809

DELIVERY ADDRESS	NAME		
	COMPANY		
	ADDRESS		
	CITY, STATE, ZIP	E MAIL	
	PHONE NUMBER (INCLUDE AREA CODE)	FAX	

PRICES AND AVAILABILITY SUBJECT TO CHANGE WITHOUT NOTICE. THIS FORM EFFECTIVE JULY 1995